MW00882098

THE INNER MIND REVISITED

By

A.L. Ward

Sr. Catherine
2/9/08

A.L. Ward

© 2002 by A. L. Ward. All rights reserved.

No part of this book may be reproduced, stored in a retrieval system, or transmitted by any means, electronic, mechanical, photocopying, recording, or otherwise, without written permission from the author.

ISBN: 1-4033-8760-5 (e-book)
ISBN: 1-4033-8761-3 (Paperback)

This book is printed on acid free paper.

1stBooks – rev. 11/26/02

Also by A.L. Ward

The Inner Mind

The how & Why of Self Hypnosis

Regression therapy and how it works

The natural way to better health

TABLE OF CONTENTS

ACKNOWLEDGMENTS

To all my friends who participated in bringing this knowledge from the other side of life.

To Julie and Marjory who spent countless hours going over my material making suggestions and corrections to give the material more meaning and clarity.

To Jean and Hazel who included me in the research project. To Loren who made it possible

DEDICATION

To Jocey

My personal Angel

PREFACE

This book is a follow-up to my book, "The Inner Mind", published in 1965. It answers the questions to the material and investigations left undone at that time. It continues to promote that all physical, emotional, and spiritual deficiencies are the result of negative emotions, and that many of these problems can be resolved in a few minutes through the process of hypnotic regression therapy.

The book promotes the concept of reincarnation and communication with the spirit world. It also takes a look at the possibility of life in other systems of the universe. The concept of reincarnation is always present in the inner mind regardless of our conscious beliefs. I have found that those who choose to be agnostics or atheists have the same spiritual awareness in the super-conscious as those who practice a religion and the belief in God.

I discovered that many people are willing to live with a diagnosis simply because they have been told it is hereditary, and we can allow the word "hereditary" to become a self-filling prophecy. In regression therapy we often find it was the individual's choice to be born into a particular family, or situation, for a specific experience necessary for growth.

During the past forty-plus years, I have shared with, and accompanied many in their subjective journeys to the Inner Mind. By my own interpretations, theories, and guidelines, I hope to help the reader to a better understanding of themselves and their widening potential so they too, might strive toward a higher level of knowledge and grace in the process of living.

FORWARD

The mind of every living thing is a history book, a record of the past, present and the future. To be able to read and understand these records depends on the interest, purpose and privilege of the student. It is clear that man is operating with only a minimal fraction of his possibilities. What is the purpose of the unused human capability? What is its destination?.

J.B. Priestly, in his classic "Man Time" posed a riddle of the middle ages. "How many Angels can dance on the point of a needle?" He warned that there is a tendency to assume that which science finds unable to answer must not be asked at all.

Fantastic advances have been made on materialistic assumptions that are often dismissed for the lack of an hypothesis is evidence that the mind and soul are more than just a function of the brain.

Traditions, such as philosophy, religion and the humanities have forever been concerned with evolution of consciousness. Plato, Aristotle, Descartes, Kant and Hegel, a few of the greatest mental giants humanity has produced, labored with the eternal and unfathomable mysteries which still remain unanswered to the satisfaction of the physical sciences. Freud, Jung, Wundt, and many modern day psychologists have expounded differences in their interpretations of the nature of man. Higher religions surviving in this century of the Christian era are variations on a single theme, each professing to reflect insight giving a distinctive meaning and mission of its own. Great religious spokesmen of the western world, Christ, Luther, Constantine, Smith, Holms, and many others, have taught doctrines avowing the one and only true way of life.

The range of our information or understanding is gained through experience and association, as well as our ability to think outside of common belief systems. Those persons who have given to the world unusual and important knowledge are those thinkers, unafraid of being different in their beliefs and actions.

We are all different. Each soul is unique if form, with different experience and knowledge that should be shared with others. It is through the process of hypnotism that we can express and share the information of our past and present. It is through the process of hypnotism that we can explore the future.

Being created with free agency (freedom of thought) there can be no predestination as such, and yet things can be predictable. The scientific discovery of DNA (Deoxyribonucleic Acid) has shown a molecular basis of heredity. Our size, shape, looks etc, are the result of the genetic structure of our parents and ancestors. I believe the DNA is also a blueprint of a predetermined plan for our physical experience. Some things are planned in spirit to be experienced physically that cannot, or will not, be changed once the physical experience has started.

Meditation, Para-physics, Psychic Plant and Dream Research, Biofeedback, Holistic Medicine, and renewed interest in the Eastern Philosophies, such as Yoga and Mind Control, may be a part of our Evolution, that the range of man's own innate consciousness has come forth in attaining a style and respectability of its own. It would be a mistake to think of hypnotism as an "Occult" faculty. It is not. It is the power to grasp reality, and to unite the segregations of the mind, conscious, subconscious and super-conscious.

Psychic development can play an important role in helping people become conscious of their participation in the continuing miracle of creation. It is a major element in a formula for expanding human minds, transforming society, and implementing nature in the great work of evolving the human race to a higher potential.

Chapter One
WHAT IS HYPNOTISM?

Over forty years have passed since the experience that led to my continuing involvement with the mysteries of the mind. I was a police officer on patrol duty in San Bernardino, California, the night I received a radio call to check the trouble in the southwest area of the city. My partner and I found a man seated in an easy chair, his hands gripping its arms, his entire body straining in an unsuccessful effort to release him self from the chair.

Earlier in the evening the man had attended a wrestling match and, as part of the entertainment, one of the wrestlers asked for volunteers willing to be hypnotized. Believing that he could not be hypnotized, this man eagerly walked up to the arena. When seated, he was hypnotized and told he would be unable to get up from the chair. To his surprise he found he could not move until he was released verbally. After the show he drove home and relaxed in his favorite chair while his wife fixed coffee. As he related the experience to his wife he suddenly froze in his seated position and found himself unable to get up or even release his grip.

Understandably anxious, the man's wife phoned the arena only to be told that the wrestler-hypnotist had left for Los Angeles, a sixty-mile drive away. A person at the arena recommended she instruct her husband to wake up and rise from the chair. Should this fail he suggested putting ice cubes on the back of the man's neck. Neither idea worked. The wife phoned a doctor who informed her his working hours were from 8:00 am to 5:00 pm and told her that if her husband was still in this condition in the morning to bring him to the office.

My partner and I succeeded in prying the man loose from his chair only to find that he maintained the same strained and stiff position as if seated. We placed him back into his chair and tried to locate someone by telephone that might have some knowledge of hypnotism. We found no one to help us.

Trying my own idea I warmed a washcloth under a water tap and placed it on the man's arm. He relaxed at once and moved about freely. He was surprised and pleased to find that, despite an ailing heart, the experience of having been in a stiff and strained position for over two hours had not

1

caused any noticeable ill effects. In fact, he felt very well. During this entire incident no one seemed overly concerned or frightened; actually it was rather funny. This incident was mentioned in the <u>San Bernardino Sun,</u> but the article did not include the details that made the experience as amusing as it really was. I made no further contact with the man or his wife.

We left their home happy that we had been able to bring about a successful solution to a most unusual problem. However, the experience really excited me and I couldn't stop thinking about it. The possibilities that the mind could explore through this phenomenon called hypnotism seemed unbelievable. I was determined to learn more about it and after reading a small book on hypnotism, I was eager to find a willing subject on which to practice.

As it happened my sister-in-law, Bunny, had been exposed to hypnosis through a friend who had been helped, by hypnotism, to develop better study habits. Bunny agreed to be my subject and allowed me to attempt my first hypnotic induction. My brother Bud said he had never been able to touch Bunny's feet without her kicking and screaming and, if I could get Bunny to let him tickle her feet, he would believe in hypnosis. I successfully placed her under hypnosis and gave her the suggestion that she would have no objection to her husband tickling her feet. In the hypnotic state she did allow Bud to do this, convincing my brother and myself that the session had been successful. Though a little shaken and excited by the experience, I was also exhilarated and even more intrigued. I was determined to find a way to learn more about the phenomenon of hypnotism.

I found, in the personal column of our city newspaper, an ad offering instructions in hypnotism. Baron John Von Brenner, a well-known nightclub hypnotist, had placed the ad. A fellow detective and I went to visit the Baron at his home on the ruse of determining if he was breaking any city ordinance by operating a business there. In the course of our visit the Baron put on a demonstration of his art. My friend was so uncomfortable and frightened by the demonstration that he left the Baron's home without me. However, I did not leave until I made arrangements with the Baron to study with him and learn more about this exciting subject.

Von Brenner had credentials showing more than thirty years in the practice of hypnotism. He was a master hypnotist who began his career in stage hypnosis at a very young age in Germany. He claimed to have met and discussed hypnosis with the infamous Adolph Hitler before he (Hitler) came to power. He said Hitler first showed some interest in being

2

hypnotized, but, after thinking it over, decided that he did not want anyone to have "control over *his mind*".

I felt quite fortunate to have met this knowledgeable and dedicated man with all his years of experience in the fields of hypnotism and other psychic knowledge. I studied with Baron Von Brenner for more than three years, every night after work and on weekends. To help pay my tuition I gave him a car and other personal items. And in return, I believe, he gave me extra privileges because I was a police officer. My study consisted of written material and hands-on experience. He had other students and we practiced on each other.

I still don't know how I got away with spending so much time away from home. At the time my son was 23, my daughter was 15, and my wife was busy with household duties. The kids were indifferent to my activities, but my wife thought I was in cahoots with the devil. As the fifth of nine children I received various opinions from among my siblings. A younger brother thought hypnosis was great and an older sister had once dated a psychic and was using an Ouija Board. The three of us were considered weird by the rest of the family.

During childhood I was taken to Sunday school without knowing what religion was being taught and I remember going to a Baptist church, on my own, when I was about fourteen years of age. Religion was never forced on any of my family and, accordingly, I raised my children the same way. I was married, and baptized, in a Lutheran Church. Two weeks later the minister was fired because he could not afford a car to visit parishioners of the church. About fifteen years later my wife and I were baptized in a Calvary Baptist Church and a few weeks later, the minister was asked to leave his church because he gave a sermon on adultery. These actions seemed to indicate that politics were more important in religion than teaching and living the words of God. As a result we never joined another church. Furthermore, after my involvement in hypnotism, my wife was embarrassed to go to church because she feared what the minister, or other church members, would think of us. A few of my co-workers at the police department also suggested that I might be doing the work of the devil. As for myself, I believe the use of this process we call hypnotism has given me more spiritual knowledge than any religion could ever have provided. I believe organized religion sometimes gets in the way of one's own spiritual growth.

As a student my interest was directed toward stage hypnosis. My friends and I would find someone who would volunteer to be hypnotized and then cause them to react in a ridiculous, funny and entertaining manner, always taking care that the subject not be offended in any manner by the experience. I was sometimes more amazed than my audience by some of the things I could get my subjects to do, both mentally and physically. Surprising reactions slowly took form and evolved into deeper and more universal meaning. Hypnosis turned out to be a key to discoveries that continuously, to this day, open new vistas of mystic realization. The parlor trick became a wonder of the inner mind. My question was, how real is this complex phenomenon and what more and better uses can be done with it?

One of my subjects, Norm, was told to look at a non-existent clock on a blank wall behind him. He did so, and then told me what time it was. An onlooker might have said that Norm's "clock" was only a figment of his imagination, an artificial suggestion. But to harbor this attitude would miss the essence of the demonstration. There really was no clock, one could say. But for Norm, perceiving through hypnotic consciousness, and subjective reality, the clock was there. Did Norm's clock have any less validity than a glass-faced wall-piece? Remember, his "clock" told him the correct time, any time and every time.

Barbara brought Norm to one of my classes. Both were members of "Parents Without Partners", having lost their mates through death and divorce. At that time they were not even good friends. Barbara had attended my classes before and thought we could help Norm overcome his sadness over the death of his wife. One night, while using Norm for a hypnotic demonstration, I gave him a suggestion that whenever Harold, another attendee, spoke his voice would be irritating. I also suggested that when Barbara spoke her voice would be like sweet music to his ears. When I brought Norm out of hypnosis, he had no awareness of what suggestions I had given him. Harold asked Norm what he thought of being hypnotized. Norm replied, "Harold, I wish you would shut up. Your voice irritates me". Then Barbara said, "Why are you acting this way? Harold didn't say anything offensive". Norm leaned toward her and asked her to repeat what she had said and a few minutes later he was whispering in Barbara's ear trying to get her to leave the class early so they could be alone. Two weeks later they announced their plans to marry. The others in the class accused me of being responsible for this happy event.

Characteristically, nothing sounds ridiculous to a hypnotic subject because of preconceptions of ordinary awareness. The "why-should-its" and "this-is-absurd" critical conscious controls are suspended and the mind short-circuits learned behavioral constraints. Hypnosis is infinitely more than a stage trick or a "weird" experience. It is more than an altered state of reality and I believe it should be viewed as a specialized or extraordinary state. Ordinarily, what one thinks of as "consciousness" constitutes the full range of everyday existence. Any shift from one state of mind to another is an altered state and the number of shifts a person undergoes each day is countless.

Since the beginning of recorded history there have been reports that particular psychical conditions were induced in human beings by certain physical processes. The laying on of the hands, steady gazing at stones, crystals and other objects were practiced by the Egyptian and Oriental peoples for religious and medical purposes. From ancient times hypnosis has been classified by many names and interpretations. Some call it suggestion, some concentration, some persuasion, and even, as one medical journal put it, "that nasty little science".

Hypnotism is such an extraordinary phenomenon that no completely satisfactory definition has ever been developed. Debates still rage over its exact nature. The British and the American Medical Associations have defined hypnotism, in part, as "a temporary condition of altered attention, in the subject, that may be induced by another person but there is still much about hypnosis to be understood". Although the condition resembles normal sleep researchers have found that the brain wave patterns of hypnotized subjects are much closer to the patterns of deep relaxation. Thus, rather than being just a mystical phenomenon, hypnosis is generally viewed as a form of attentive, receptive, highly focused concentration in which external or peripheral events are omitted or disregarded.

Professional people now commonly accept that hypnosis is a mental attitude based on a combination of belief, faith, confidence, purpose and expectancy on the part of both the hypnotist and the subject. The combination of these factors tends to produce an attitude of increased susceptibility to suggestion on the part of the subject. When belief, faith, purpose, sincerity, emotions, and other factors are put together they form the basis that determines the effectiveness of the process known as hypnotism.

Doctor James Braid invented the term "hypnosis" in the nineteenth century. In experiments with therapeutic magnetism (also known as Mesmerism or animal magnetism), Doctor Braid confused the state of his patients' physical relaxation with sleep and coined the word "hypnotism" from the Greek word "hypnos", which means sleep. When many patients told him they had heard every word he said he tried to change the terminology but it was too late. The word hypnotism had already entered the English language and become common usage.

One thing agreed upon by students, and practitioners of hypnosis is that the process involves different levels of consciousness, most often identified as conscious, subconscious, and super-conscious. The best description I have found concerning the different levels of consciousness came from a subject during a pre-life regression session. When I asked her to identify the difference between the levels of consciousness her answer was, "Your conscious mind is what you do, your subconscious mind is what you are, and your super-conscious (the soul) is God". Could this be the same as the Trinity, mind, body and spirit?

Jung stated, "In the deepest trance state, the subconscious reaches out to the super-conscious, or Soul, and receives, from the universal unconsciousness, knowledge and wisdom. Images and thoughts completely divorce from the activity of the subject's personal life".

It is interesting to compare this twentieth-century statement with Saint Thomas Aquinas on the nature of the soul in his <u>Summa Theologies</u>, written in the thirteenth-century: "God is effectively the life both of the Spirit by charity and of the body by the Soul."

Plato, in the <u>Phaedo</u>, drew a fundamental distinction between soul and body and believed the soul to have three parts: simple, non-composite and eternal. According to the Christian belief in Trinity, man is composed of body, soul, and spirit. The great seventeenth-century German astronomer, Johannes Keplar, asserted that there are not more, and not fewer, than three dimensions of space as it compares with the Trinity. Three has symbolic form, as do the levels of consciousness in the hypnotic state: light, cataleptic, and somnambulistic.

The hypnotist should establish between himself and the subject an emotional bond of confidence, sympathy, liking and cooperation, so the relationship is, in itself, suggestive of beneficial results. There must be an element of rapport between the hypnotist and the subject. We put the various constructive elements of the subject's personality to work. Healthy emotions will over-ride, or remold, the destructive emotions which are responsible for negative mental, physical, and spiritual conditions. We appeal to the ambitions, spiritual feelings, and love of self and family, patriotism, and so on. These elements are the starting points for the effort one must make to regain self-control. A new attitude toward life, on the part of the subject, must occur in order to change or adjust the condition, or purpose, at hand. If there is no change in the thought process there is no change in the condition. However, both hypnotist and subject must be strong individuals. As Albert Moll states in his book The Study of Hypnotism (1889), "The influence of one person over another is dependent on the individuality of both".

Because of the continued disagreement concerning the exact nature of hypnotism, some authorities claim that anyone is potentially hypnotizable and that failure to induce a hypnotic state is due to either poor techniques on the part of the hypnotist or resistance on the part of the subject. In contrast, there are some researchers who claim that hypnotism, as it is generally understood, does not exist at all. They believe hypnosis is not the result of some alteration in the subject's capacities or mental state but is the consequence of "role playing" based upon the subject's preconceptions of how hypnotized persons are supposed to behave.

Hypnosis is a natural part of human behavior although persons involved in its practice and studies do not agree on the exact reason or cause. The state of hypnosis has been described as a narrowed, or selective, conscious condition similar to a dream state or trance, or a condition of exaggerated suggestibility. It is important to differentiate applied or self-hypnosis from other states of altered awareness such as sleep, intoxication, sedation, or tranquilization. In sleep, for example, all channels of sensory input are inhibited from critical awareness. In hypnosis, on the other hand, there is a conscious awareness of what is occurring in the external presence and the reality of what is occurring in the mind. There can be no denial of the dual character of the mind. Unlike the conscious mind, the subconscious is subject to control by suggestion on certain levels and is incapable of inductive reasoning. Once the subconscious mind has been reached suggestions put to it become truth unless these suggestions violate natural instincts of self-preservation and perpetuation of the human race. The three different levels of hypnosis, and the purpose, determine the results of the session.

When I was taught about applying hypnotism I learned that the most important condition was confidence on the part of the hypnotist, and this attitude was gained and strengthened by knowledge. Personally, I found that knowledge came easily as the result of this belief and, with believing, came sincerity and purpose. I learned there were no limitations to the abilities of the mind and body to respond within the laws of their natures and that the mind retains memory of every impression and experience of the human senses since the beginning of its existence.

Rapport between the hypnotist and subject is determined by attitudes of trust, purpose, and belief. This rapport also determines the success of any induction. A state of hypnosis is accomplished when the subject's conscious attitude is passive (letting it happen) and communication is established with the subconscious. This is made possible by suggestion coupled with psychological conditioning, resulting in the belief that the suggestion will, or has, become true. It is a proven fact that someone new to hypnosis may be more successful than a person with years of experience, simply because of the harmony between people.

What can be accomplished in the somnambulistic stage cannot be accomplished in the light, or cataleptic, attitudes. However, I have found the mind will automatically assume the proper level of consciousness to recover whatever information is requested if the proper rapport has been established with the subject. The fact that the subconscious mind has absolute control of the functions, conditions, and sensations of the body makes possible the complete reflection (expressions) of the powers of the mind and body within the scope of their individual natures. I promote the idea that the conscious, subconscious, and super-conscious are separate and independent functions; they can, and do, operate independently and simultaneously. The best physical existence is when these systems think and act alike. Man's true nature, of course, is of the soul. Therefore, the conscious and subconscious should be compatible to the super-conscious (soul) system.

The induction of hypnosis is done by as many different methods and techniques as there are persons involved in its practice. When I started learning about hypnotism most hypnotic inductions were done with words. I am now convinced that hypnosis is more of a mental process than a verbal process. It is my belief that hypnotism is simply a process of communication. We can communicate by words, touch, looks, and the non-contact manipulation of the body energies. Behind these expressions is the power of thought. A concentrated look, a touch, and energy manipulation, make it easier to convey the thought and words make the thought more effective. All responses to hypnosis are to some degree different. Not all people will respond to mental communication. This is not because they don't receive the thought but because they don't know how, or if, to respond to the thought so words sometime become necessary.

I do not now, nor have I ever used mechanical devices. Lights, hypnotic discs, medallions, or other objects used as a point of concentration are unnecessary. As far as I am concerned there are only two requirements needed to cause the hypnotic attitude. (1) No one can be hypnotized unless he has the idea he is going to be. (2) It is also true that certain subjects cannot resist because their willpower is weakened by fear or by the idea of a superior power that can influence them in spite of themselves. It is certain that anyone who does not want to be hypnotized, and who knows that he need not be influenced if he does not wish to be, can successfully resist every attempt. Once the subject believes that what you say or do will happen the rest is easy. Hypnotism is simply an attitude of belief by the subject, and the hypnotist, in the method or process of communication.

Hypnotic induction begins during an exploratory interview which provides the hypnotist with information as to the best method of approach for the particular subject. For example, about one in five persons are highly suggestible. This can be determined by observing the eyes and other body signs during the interview. There are also simple methods of testing to determine the personality and potential reaction to the hypnotic process. A common hypnotic formula is made up of certain words which, when given in the manner of suggestion, cause the subject to respond to the hypnotic state. The mind is trained to interpret words that cause a physical reaction and, therefore, will react to such words as <u>sleep</u>, <u>down</u>, <u>heavy</u>, <u>deeper</u>, and so forth.

These words all have their place in an induction of hypnosis by this method. As the subject begins to respond with sensations of increasing relaxation and drowsiness (processes normally associated with the beginning of sleep) he enters into a specific state between wakefulness and normal sleep. The feeling is of weightlessness, or floating, accompanied by a sensation of numbness, or "sans souci" (without care). One may believe he could move about freely now if he so chooses but he will not, because he does not seem to want to.

Many people think that, in hypnosis, they will lose control and become slaves of the hypnotist. The truth is that those who submit to hypnosis can do as they wish, but they don't want to, preferring to go along with what's happening. The subjects are motionless and their appearance to the casual onlooker is deceptive. The mind is alert, and communication at this point is between the hypnotist and the subject's subconscious. It is in this relaxed non-critical stage that the skilled hypnotist can selectively focus the subject's awareness or attention. The subject can eventually recognize this state, and with practice, direct the process autonomously, creating self-hypnosis.

The mind is amazing in its prodigious memory. After the proper hypnotic attitude is obtained the mind, by direction, can recall any moment of its past and can also recall the instant of changes in mental, physical, and spiritual attitudes. It is by this method that physical and emotional disorders and negative habits, caused by a prior mental attitude, can be corrected. For examples of this I refer you to the chapter on case histories in this book. The pattern further discloses that a mental link exists between physical existence and a spiritual origin and destination and that there are laws, which govern the process of one's soul to an ultimate goal.

It was during my first experience with hypnotic age regression that I became aware that hypnotism had a much greater potential than just making someone do amusing things. There was the expression of communication between the physical and spiritual worlds; the exchange of information and knowledge relating to events not yet experienced by the physical senses. I am referring to the idea of predestination and other psychic expressions.

Once I started working with the deeper consciousness of the mind little else seemed to matter but to research the causes and reactions of this phenomenon. I spent the next several years doing hypnotic regressions, tape-recording every session. I compared, I challenged, and I cross-examined the subjects in an effort to learn the truth of what was being said by each person I worked with. During my years of investigation of hypnotic regressions I found recurring patterns. People can respond with psychic knowledge, which is beyond their awareness in the normal state of consciousness and beyond the hypnotist's suggestive guidance. Laws that govern this phenomenon seem to operate independently on an entirely different plane from ordinary wakefulness or the lighter stages of hypnosis. Subjects in this hypnotic attitude can describe an existence in another life. They will also describe an existence between these lives, this being a spiritual realm. There is a disassociation of personality and the experience seems to flow from within, over which the subjects have not the slightest control, and though they may profess to have no memory of the incident there is a reaction, or result. Once a person experiences a pre-natal awareness of the spiritual realm, and even though there is no conscious awareness of the event, there is a sensation of serenity experienced in the physical conscious attitude of the subject at the conclusion of the experience.

The following are some of the expressions I have found are always present in a pre-natal regression.

- Some unity or identity exists and it is not affected by what is commonly known as death.

- A design, pattern, or purpose for one's existence is evident, a purpose which extends beyond one's present life.

- A goal exists toward which one is evolving.

- A value standard is perceived (something is better than something else and that something is best of all) and the goal is the highest value against which all other values are measured.

- That which is meaningful in experiences, for the particular individual, is retained and determines what he is.

- Experience tends to be absolute and not relative and circumstances and their effect upon the individual are self-contained within the confines of that individual.

- This system also implies a principle of justice. Life then, with all its inequalities, receives its reason and acceptance.

- This system also implies an element of accepted proof, a standard against which reality is determined and defined.

- There is an element of belief; something is accepted outside of normally accepted knowledge.

- Finally, fate takes on new meaning involving free will and the mechanism of choice.

The mind not only contains the knowledge of life, and the purpose for its existence and conduct, but contains the answers for its own improvement of emotional, physical, and spiritual conditions. The human mind retains billions of thought impressions. It has been shown that, under certain conditions, a person can recall past experiences by his own efforts. The mind, like a computer, registers and retains everything experienced within the awareness of the senses, conscious or subconscious, to be available for recall at a future time. In the state of hypnosis, where the mind is free of distraction and a concentration of thought is created, the individual can, without hesitation, recall anything having occurred in his lifetime. This recall can be in the form of memory alone or the individual can be placed in a state of mind where the recall is as if he were actually reliving the experience to the minutest detail of observance.

Hypnotic regression, which produces the phenomenon of the subject describing an existence prior to birth into this present life, also shows that existence is continuous from the creation of that entity. Of all the many persons I have regressed I have never failed to get a description of an existence that was prior to being born into the present life. This existence may contain one or several past lives, including the purpose for each life, and the existence of life in a spiritual realm between each of these lives. Whenever a subject says he has lived more than one hundred past lives I find that most of those lives have been lived in other planetary systems. It is rare that a subject has lived more than fifteen past lives on the earth plane. Those who have lived lives in other systems always feel different while in the earth environment and this includes their reactions to the people in their life. The information and knowledge given by subjects, while in the spiritual realm, contains all the knowledge gained during the total life cycles of experiences, past and present, and can offer insight into the future.

In regression, whenever a certain point in time is reached, the person will identify himself with his existence at that time and we have a change of identity, a different name, a different area and, almost always, a change in nationality. From all appearances there emerges an altogether different person. There are those who say that these different personalities are "autonomous creations of the unconscious", types of split personalities, or memories of someone or something about which they have read or may have seen in a movie. There are those who suppose the person has tuned into un-evolved spirits and/or energy fields, and others who believe hypnotic regressions to be proof of reincarnation. There are also some who search for larger truths and, in the quest, sense the joy of immortality.

To quote Doctor David F. Tracy in his book How to Use Hypnosis (1952), "There is probably no way in which we can learn about the human mind so quickly, so thoroughly, and so interestingly as through the study and practice of hypnotism".

Chapter Two
HISTORY OF HYPNOTISM

This book is not intended to be an instruction guide to hypnotism or to offer a complete history of its origin and practice. However, inasmuch as this book deals mainly with hypnotic techniques, I feel it is necessary to give some background about its beliefs and practice. The names, dates and history, to which I refer, are to give the reader a better chance to evaluate my personal experiences and opinions.

Hypnotism is not new. It has, in some form or another, been known since the earliest of times. It was practiced by the Egyptians, Persians, Greeks, and Indians, and has been employed by priests, mystics and soothsayers, as well as fakirs and charlatans. As recorded In the Bible, Naaman was supposed to have referred to animal magnetism when he said to Elisha's messenger, "I thought He will surely come out to me, and stand, and call on the name of the Lord, his God, and strike his hand over the place and recover the Leper" (II Kings 5:11). The original Hebrew, I believe, could be rendered, "Move his hand up and down over the place".

Hypnotism appeared in the United States in the form of animal magnetism, Mesmerism, Electro-biology, and Electro-psychology, among many others. Von Helmon (1577-1644) wrote an essay, titled "Magnetic Cure of Wounds", in which he described the use of magnetic hypnotism to effect medical cures. In 1646, Father Kircher described his experiments on animals in which he produced a kind of catalepsy. The "Ghost Dances" of the American Indian seem to have consisted of producing hypnosis by dancing in a circle, always compatible with the earth moving on its axis. In Turkey a, "Whirling Dervish" produces a similar effect.

Freidrich Anton Mesmer (1734-1815) graduated as a doctor in 1766, defending a thesis on "The Influence of the Planets on the Human Body". He settled in Paris, France, about 1778, and soon created a furor because of the wonderful cures that he allegedly effected by means of magnetism. He publicly asserted that his treatment was of universal applicability and that his discoveries would "enable the physician to decide upon the health of every individual, and the presence of the diseases to which many may be exposed." In this way, he thought, the art of healing might be brought to absolute perfection.

Mesmer surrounded his treatment with a great deal of impressive mystery. His patients assembled in a large, dimly and religiously lighted, room while from an adjoining area came the enchanting sounds of music. In the center of the patient's room stood a large tub containing bottles from which iron rods were stretched outwardly. The patients held these rods while they gazed upon the bottles. Cords, or wires, connected the patients to one another. Mesmer, himself, walked around the room carrying an iron rod with which to magnetize special patients or would make a stroking motion with his hands or use what we call "fascination" (as by a fixed look).

Early in his career Mesmer was interested in astrology believing that the planets exerted an influence on the health of human beings. He first thought this influence was electrical but later referred to it as magnetism which he called "animal magnetism". He achieved great notoriety for curing diseases by first, making passes over the affected areas of the body with magnets and, afterwards, by manipulation or stroking the diseased bodies. These cures, he believed, were caused by a fluid, active in the human nervous system, enabling one person to exert an influence over another by transference of this invisible fluid. Many wonderful cures were affected by his methods and these were brought to the attention of the medical profession which ridiculed and condemned Mesmer and his practice. In 1784, by order of King Louis XVI, a government commission was appointed to inquire into his pretensions. The report was adverse asserting, among other things, that "There is nothing to prove the existence of the animal magnetism fluid", and that "All treatment in public, in which magnetism is employed must, in the end, be productive of evil results". Finally, the Prussian Government adopted Mesmer's techniques for hospital treatment and in 1817 passed a law confining the use of magnetism in Prussia to medical men.

DuPotet began a series of observations in 1820, and in 1825 the French Academy of Medicine appointed another commission to re-examine the claims of animal magnetism. The report of this commission concluded, "Some of the magnetized patients experienced no benefit". In one case, "habitual suffering was suspended," in another, "strength returned," in a third, "epileptic attacks were averted for several months," and in a fourth, "serious paralysis of long standing was completely cured". About 1837 DuPotet went to London, England, and made the acquaintance of Dr. John Elliotson, who was at the time physician to the University College Hospital. Elliotson was so impressed by what Du Potet showed him that he adopted magnetism into his regular practice. The council of the University College passed a resolution forbidding the use of Mesmerism in their hospital causing Elliotson to give up his post there because he refused to submit to their dictation.

James Esdaile (1808-1859) graduated in 1830 as a medical doctor. Dr. Esdaile went to Calcutta in the service of the East India Company in 1831 where he was given charge of the Hooghly Hospital. On April 14, 1845, he performed his first experiment with Mesmerism on a Hindu convict. Esdaile left Calcutta June 1, 1851, having recorded 261 painless operations performed by the aid of Mesmerism including such major cases as a lithotomy, amputations, and the removal of large tumors in Elephantiasis. Further investigation of the phenomena by a few scientific men found that they could develop the power of clairvoyance and other psychic phenomena in their subjects. They caused their subjects to obey mental orders, healed the sick, caused the lame to walk, and the blind to see.

To James Braid, a Manchester surgeon, the honor is now generally accorded for having rescued Mesmerism from the region of quackery and of endeavoring to secure it a recognized place in medicine. In the year 1841, Braid undertook to demonstrate that the theory of magnetic fluid had nothing to do with the production of the so-called sleep and so, to put an end to such pretensions, proposed that the term "hypnotism" should replace Mesmerism and animal magnetism. In 1843, he published a book dealing with the subject. He claimed to have found hypnotism useful in cases of rheumatism, epilepsy, paralysis, neuralgia, palpitations, etc. However, the great body of the medical profession did not seem to have taken kindly to hypnotism and so, when chloroform was introduced, it thrust hypnotic anesthesia into the shadows and Braid's work was quickly forgotten and the therapeutic possibilities of hypnotism were completely ignored.

Dr. Braid's method was to have a person concentrate upon an object being held before his eyes. There are those who have their subjects look at blinking lights of different colors or watch a disc designed to cause the eyes to tire and lose focus. There have been machines designed to emit high and low frequency sounds, which cause the mind to assume a trance-like state and, there is the use of drugs.

In 1850, there were "Mesmeric Infirmaries" operating in Bristol and London, apparently conducted solely by laymen. One claimed to have cured many of the "incurables" of the regular hospitals including cases of deafness, and chronic rheumatism. Other investigations into the phenomena by Bernheim, Moll, Charcot, Bramwell, and Schrenck-Notizing continued the research of Mesmerism and hypnotism. Schools were established which differed in both theory and practice. The following three examples are the leading points of difference in these schools.

1. The theory of the school at Nancy, founded by Doctor Liebault, was that the physiological condition, characterizing the hypnotic state, was determined by mental action alone and that the phenomena could be produced best in persons of sound physical health and perfect mental balance.

2. The Paris school, founded by Professor Charcot, held that hypnotism was the result of an abnormal or diseased condition of the nerves and that the true hypnotic condition could be produced only in persons whose nerves were diseased, independent of suggestion in any form.

3. The Mesmerist school held to the fluid theory of Mesmer that the hypnotic condition was induced, independent of suggestion, by passes made by the operator over the subject, accompanied by intense concentration of the mind and will of the operator and, that from him flowed a fluid which impinged upon the subject where it was directed producing therapeutic, or other effects, in obedience to the will of the operator. It was believed that these effects could be best obtained by personal contact even though they could be produced at a distance without the knowledge of the subject and, without suggestion.

Each school presented facts, which seemed to support its theory but it will be evident that no school was entirely right. In addition, investigators have always been at odds as to the causes and results of the hypnotic phenomena. The attitude of the medical profession toward Mesmer, in particular, both in 1775, and today, has been particularly harsh. When book one The Inner Mind was published in 1966, a medical specialist warned, in a local paper, "Psychotics are the very first to volunteer for hypnosis, and can be harmed permanently by it. It can take away their defenses against psychosis leaving them permanently and hopelessly insane". Some medical specialists still refuse to discuss the topic of hypnosis because it represents a method of healing about which they know nothing and care little about or because of personal hang-ups against its use.

Before 1850, there was almost no scientific attempt to explain the things people actually did or what association the mind, or mental process, had to do with the physical. It was in 1879, that a German Psychologist, Wilhelm Wundt, established the world's first psychological laboratory.

Sigmund Freud (1856-1939), founder of psychoanalysis, created a method called "free association" to study the unconscious factors in the personality. The patient would lie on a couch, close his eyes and relax letting his mind wander freely and, from time to time, tell the analyst about what he was thinking. By well directed questions the analyst tried to make the patient remember, and tell about, experiences in his past, which he had repressed and which might lie at the bottom of his problem. This was usually done while the patient was in a conscious state of mind.

William James, in describing "mystical states", stated they are never merely "interruptive". "Some memory of their content always remains as well as a profound sense of their importance. They modify the inner life of the subject." And so they do.

Today hypnotism and Mesmerism are sometimes deemed to be interchangeable, as meaning the same process. They are not. The Mesmerist used intense thought and "magnetic passes" to effect a cure of their patients. The hypnotist relied on verbal suggestion alone. Because the method of the hypnotist was easier and seemed to be just as effective as Mesmerism, the techniques of Mesmerism were neglected. We now have ample evidence to prove the transference of thought between life forms, i.e., mental telepathy. We also know that the "invisible fluid" spoken of by Mesmer is recognized now as body energies (the aura) which can, and do, affect other bodies and this energy can be directed, as can thought, to a specific person for a specific purpose.

Our oldest records of antiquity indicate that wise men everywhere knew and understood the applications of these principles. The first great minds used these in the application of their professions and to build the foundations of many great civilizations, which have passed through recorded history.

The legends of antiquity, handed down by different races tell us of these inner powers and their applications to the many arts, thereby raising mankind above all other creatures on this earth. We are also informed by legends that, because these inner powers can be applied for the good or evil of mankind they have been shrouded in mystery and veiled from the eyes of the unworthy awaiting that time when man has raised himself to the spiritual level whereby he understands this power. In their endeavor to conceal this knowledge from the unworthy the ancient wise men formed themselves into brotherhoods, priesthoods, and other schools of thought. They handed down this knowledge from one generation to the next by word of mouth or in writings concealed in symbolisms so that only those who possessed the inquiring mind and desire for knowledge would find the key and open the doorway to these mysteries of antiquity.

Age regression, used in hypnotism, is a tool (key) by which the door to the mind may be opened. It remains for the person with a desire for knowledge and an inquiring mind to enter the realm of many wonderful experiences of health and happiness. Hypnotic age regression approaches will be covered, in detail, in the next chapter.

History has shown hypnotism can be a very effective tool in establishing physical and emotional health in the human body. Because hypnotism is a process of communication between different personalities there cannot be the consistency demanded by science in its use. We don't know how affective we can be with hypnotism until we try.

Chapter Three
THERAPY CASE HISTORIES

In 1968, I was associated with a group of chiropractors using hypnosis to assist persons to lose weight, stop smoking, and overcome other undesirable habits. One day a woman came into the office hardly able to walk. She used two canes as she shuffled, or slid, her feet along the floor. She came to lose weight and had a secondary problem with arthritis.

During my consultation with her she stated that her doctor had said if she didn't lose weight immediately she would be dead within a month and determining the method of doing this was her problem. The same doctor was also treating her for the arthritic condition and, over a period of seven years, she had been given a variety of pills to ease the pain. On her monthly visit the doctor would enquire of her which type pill was most effective for the pain and would then give her the prescription of her choice, most of the time without any examination. She commented on how she spent her days and nights at home in a rocking chair and how she slept only from 1:00A.M. to 4:00A.M. every night because of the pain she was experiencing. She also said that she customarily took at least eight Valium or Darvon pills each day.

I set a schedule to see her three times a week, each session to last about thirty minutes, and it was during one hypnotic session that she told me her illness started two years after she and her present husband married. He had been in the United States Air Force at the time of their marriage and they both had children from previous marriages. It was for this reason her husband's mother was against their marriage. A few days following they're wedding her husband received orders to transfer overseas so arrangements were made for her husband's family to visit them at their home.

At the time of their arrival she was in the kitchen preparing dinner. Her mother-in-law, upon entering the house, came directly to her in the kitchen, struck her across the chest and stated, "You will never be a woman to my son and he will never be a man to you". The mother-in-law then turned and left the room. Knowing how this woman felt about the marriage she said and did nothing about the incident.

Her sister-in-law, having witnessed this confrontation, told the woman she had observed what her mother had done and asked why. My client said she told the sister-in-law it was just a misunderstanding and to forget about it. The sister-in-law said that her mother was known as a witch where they lived in Central California and she was thought to have been responsible for the death of a man in their town. My client told me she had forgotten about the incident herself and recalled it only in hypnosis when she was directed to relate to the origin and cause of her condition.

She said her husband's assignment overseas lasted two years during which time she maintained their home and was well and happy except for the fact that her husband was not there with her. On the day he returned home she became ill and as time passed her condition worsened and, after seven years, she was in the condition that brought her to my office.

As our sessions continued she would tell me how much she had improved, how she was able to go to town and shop and how she no longer had to rely on the pain pills. She was now able to sleep a full eight to ten hours a night or nap in the afternoon without the interruption of pain. She described the sensation of the hypnotic attitude as feeling as if she were being submerged in a bath of warm oil. Her body joints were becoming more flexible, less swollen, and nearly free of pain. The method I used for the first few sessions was to simply suggest the joint areas would become warm and the body nerve systems would stimulate the affected areas. The improvement, after the first week, was such that she chose to walk to her home a few blocks from my office and her family thought some stimulating drug had brought about this improvement.

During a session in the third week she remarked that she and her mother-in-law had become good friends over the past nine years and they visited often but that the incident of their first meeting had never been discussed. During another session she spoke of plans to visit her in-laws during a holiday weekend and, on learning of the intended visit, I conceived an idea that proved to resolve her condition. While she was in hypnosis I suggested that upon her arrival at the home of her mother-in-law she should confront her about their first meeting. She was to remind her of the slapping and tell her the incident had been forgiven and she felt no resentment toward her. I also gave her a post-hypnotic suggestion that she would not remember being told to take this action.

At our next session she arrived at my office radiant and full of life. She wore a new dress and her hair was newly styled. She was without any support to walk and her excitement was overwhelming as she told everyone in the office of her visit with her husband's family.

Upon arrival at their home she had had a compulsion to confront her mother-in-law about her actions at their first meeting. The moment she confessed that the incident didn't matter anymore she felt a wonderful relief come over her body as if a tremendous weight had been lifted from her. That night she and her husband went dancing.

When they were preparing to return home her mother-in-law came to her, put her arms around her and wished her well, stating she was sure there would be no further problems. My clients life had, for the past nine years, been void of sexual activity. Following her recovery this condition also adjusted itself to a most satisfying conclusion. I had no further contact with this woman. I did see her on the street and working in her yard. She had trimmed down considerably and she moved with strength and vigor. I learned she had also taken a job in town.

This is an example of a physical ailment being caused by a mental or emotional expression and, by changing the emotional attitude, changed the physical condition. The emotion caused by the slapping incident coupled with the suggestion, "You will never be a woman to my son and he will never be a man to you" had created in her subconscious an emotional response to the suggestion thereby causing the physical condition and making the suggestion become real.

In 1968, it took a number of sessions over three weeks to resolve the problem. Today, by using my present method, the problem could have been resolved in one session of less than an hour.

It has been noted that my first interest in hypnotism was to find people who would submit to demonstrations of my newly acquired powers of hypnosis enabling me to cause these volunteers to react to my commands without question. After I became proficient in my methods of induction my interest turned to the study and investigation of hypnotic age regression. The process and the result of age regression increased my knowledge and desire to use my abilities of hypnosis to help others in their search to find emotional, physical, and spiritual comfort. It was this desire that led me to the medical group and my involvement in religious studies. I have tried to demonstrate, in everything I do, that anyone can overcome the adverse conditions affecting the three essential conditions of life: i.e. mental, physical, and spiritual fulfillment.

The following are examples of physical deficiencies resulting from an accumulation, or intensity, of negative imprints. The reconstruction of these past negative emotions improved or resolved the physical condition.

FEMALE REPRODUCTION SYSTEM

In the Parks Research and Education Project (PREP, Refer to page 25) a young lady came to evaluate a problem in her reproduction system. She mentioned she had already had a partial hysterectomy but was still having pain in her vagina. Under hypnosis it was determined that the cause was associated with the emotion of guilt connected to sexual expressions. We determined the origin of this emotion as having occurred at about the age of twelve. I had her mentally reconstruct this experience to a positive expression. We then came forward in her life, determined and reconstructed all of the negative emotional experiences. She was then told her mind could see the present condition of the reproductive system and to make the necessary repairs. She described a cyst, about an inch in diameter which had formed on the remaining part of this system. While she was reconstructing the negative emotion to a positive expression she experienced the sensation of warm fluid flowing from the cyst. She mentally observed it shrink and vanish.

About two years later she called to tell me she had married. She had become pregnant but because of her reproductive system being partially removed, she couldn't carry the pregnancy to full term.

Following the publication of my first book I received a call from a lady who said she had a story for me if I ever wrote another book. She told me that a few years ago she was about to have a hysterectomy because of having several miscarriages. One night, prior to the planned surgery, a voice came into her mind and asked if she would like to have a baby girl. She responded by thinking, "yes, but I haven't been able to give birth". This inner voice assured her that everything would be all right. She cancelled the surgery and soon afterwards became pregnant. This baby was carried full term without any problems such as morning sickness, and she gave birth to a girl. When this child was about two years old they were having breakfast together when the girl said, "You're better than my other mother". When the lady asked what her daughter meant the girl replied, "My other mother used to beat me. One morning we were eating breakfast and my mother beat me so bad I decided to die. Now I'm with you". This story is typical of expressions in past life therapy.

Another young lady in the Research Program came to me with information that she had not had a menstrual period for over five years. Medical people had suggested she might have a brain tumor even though she showed no signs of a physical or emotional deficiency. The hypnotherapy approach to the situation determined a problem in her marriage. At the start of their married life her husband had made it very clear he didn't like kids and they weren't going to have any. A short time later she separated from her husband and the day her divorce was final she started having her period.

She has since remarried and now has two children. When her second child was three years old he began talking about a past life as a truck driver with two daughters, "down Texas way". At about the age of five he stopped talking about this experience because his older brother kept telling him he was crazy. It is common for children to talk of imaginary friends and about past lives. Due to the lack of understanding by their parents, siblings, and friends, they move away from the awareness simply because they don't want to feel they are different.

EMPHYSEMA

This next case relates to Murphy, a watchmaker in the city where I worked. We met at his shop to which I had taken my watch for repair. During our conversation I told him of my book, The Inner Mind, which had just been published and before I left his shop he purchased one of them. When I returned for my watch a few days later he mentioned that he had enjoyed reading my book. He said that religion had not shown him much during his life and my book made sense to him by explaining some of his feelings and beliefs. We had only a brief discussion before I had to leave.

It was several months later that, while at work, I received a call from Murphy's wife. She was at a hospital with her husband where he had been a patient for the past seventeen days. He was being treated for a heart condition, bleeding ulcers, and emphysema. His doctors had told them that Murphy would not live through the night and because of this dire prediction he asked his wife to call and request that I visit him at the hospital before he died. Upon arriving at the hospital I was again told of this man's condition and what his doctor had told them. As I entered his room he was having much difficulty breathing due to his emphysema and when he was able to speak, he asked me if I thought hypnotism would help him. I told him I could not interfere with his treatment and that his doctor knew what was best for him. He continued to beg me to do something, anything that would ease his pain and discomfort. Not wanting to completely ignore his appeal for help, I placed my hand on his forehead in a manner of assurance that he would be all right. He immediately relaxed, his breathing became normal, and he fell asleep and I left the room without another word. I told his wife, who had been waiting in the hall, that he was sleeping and I left the hospital.

Was it Murphy's belief that whatever I did was a part of hypnotism and would help? Was there something in my touch that caused his reaction? Maybe it was a little of both, only God knows.

The following day I received another call from Murphy's wife, who said they wanted to see me at the hospital. I thought she meant the hospital officials wanted to see me but she just meant that Murphy wanted me to come. For the first time in three weeks he had slept the entire night without awakening, and without medication. He had awakened that morning, started joking with the nurses, and now he was asking for me. I stopped by the hospital on my way home from work and found him in good spirits. He said to me, "I don't know what you did to me yesterday but I wish you would do it again". I told him I had only touched his forehead, indicating how I had done it by touching him there again. He suddenly relaxed and after a few minutes said, "See how fast it works," then fell asleep.

Two days later Murphy was released from the hospital and sent home. I visited with him several times there and each time he showed more improvement. He told me the reason he had asked for me to come to the hospital was because he thought hypnosis would ease his pain so he could die easier. He had had no thought about it making him well. Murphy lived three more years and then died from neglect and loneliness.

After returning home from the hospital he started feeling the need for sex but his wife would not allow it because she was afraid it would harm him. Murphy even tried to get the housekeeper to have sex with him, thus offending his wife. Toward the end she said Murphy would stand naked in front of the window exposing himself to anyone who passed by and because of this, she had him committed to the Patton State Hospital for the mentally ill. When I visited Murphy at the Patton Hospital he felt his wife had abandoned him and, because he had no other friends, there was no need for him to go on living. Three days later he died. It was Murphy's faith (belief) in me, and in what hypnosis might do, that took him from his deathbed. It was rejection and abandonment of his need to be wanted that killed him.

INJURED SPINAL DISC

It was in 1977, that I was chosen to participate in a research project designed to find effective and speedy methods to correct both emotional and physical problems. The Parks Research and Education Project (PREP) sponsored by the Parapsychology Association of Riverside, Inc., and funded by the Psychological Research Foundation, Inc. in Oregon, lasted three years with a five-year follow-up to the volunteer clients. Persons with previously documented medical problems which had not responded to orthodox medical procedures were invited to take part in this project at no cost to them. The project was designed to evaluate a condition, determine its origin and cause, and correct the problem by using hypnotic techniques to activate a healing process. The following are a few of my cases that related to a physical injuries which were corrected by the mental ability of the injured person.

Case Number 511-R, July 1979. My subject was a forty-year old male who had injured his lower back, when he was sixteen years of age, while helping his father lift a car engine. From that time on he had suffered from both back and leg pains. He had been medically treated for torn ligaments and sore muscles and the treatment consisted of wearing a back brace and the consumption of pills to ease this pain. He had not been able to do any physical work since the accident so his purpose of taking part in our project was to see if we were able to give him relief.

During the first hour session the subject was hypnotized and told that his mind could mentally scan the injured area and examine the extent of the injuries. He responded by saying that at the bottom of his spine there was a black spot. He described the spot as being about the size of a nickel, twice as thick, and very hard. He was then asked if he could mentally repair the injury and, at that instant, in his mind he observed a pair of hands and arms that had appeared out of nowhere and, which with a knife, began cutting open the flesh along his spine exposing this black spot. The subject said he was observing this from outside and above his body. Upon exposure the hand reached in and removed the black spot from his body. After the removal of this object the mysterious hands sewed his back where it had been cut and the mental surgery was complete.

The time in hypnosis was less than twenty minutes. He was awakened and another appointment was made for the following week. Three days later the subject called to say he didn't think any further evaluation of the problem was necessary. He had experienced soreness in both hips for two days after which he was completely free of pain. There was no restriction or discomfort as he moved furniture and did other heavy work. These were some of the things he had been unable to do since age sixteen.

He did, however, ask if I would help him with another problem that had been with him for a long time. He had a "heart flutter", an irregular heartbeat, and tightness in his chest. An appointment was confirmed for the following week.

He was again hypnotized and directed, as before, to mentally scan the problem area and describe the condition. He stated that, in a tube (blood vessel) below the aorta, there was a piece of skin attached to one side of the inner wall. When the blood flowed through the tube it caused this skin to "flutter". He then added that there would be no problem unless this skin attached itself to the other wall of the tube and stopped or restricted the flow of blood. When I asked if he could repair this condition he responded by saying, "I can't, but Sidney can". I asked him who Sidney was? and his response was, "I don't know; he's the guy who helped me with my back problem last week". I said, "Okay, let Sidney do the job and tell me what he does".

He said Sidney was cutting open his chest from about two inches above the sternum to below his rib cage on the left side and he was having trouble getting a piece of meat out of the way so he could get to the tube. Once located Sidney clamped it on either side of the problem area, cut the tube and removed the skin obstruction. After suturing the tube together Sidney put the "piece of meat" in place under the rib cage and sewed his chest together. This entire process again took less than twenty minutes. Three days later the subject called to report there had been a soreness in his chest for two days after which there were no longer any symptoms of the problem.

After talking about this case with the director of the project we decided to have the subject return so that we could video tape a re-enactment of the process. He agreed and returned the following week. We explained that the reason for this re-enactment was to make a better record of this extraordinary case. He was to be directed to re-live the experiences that had resolved the problems in his back and chest.

When he entered hypnosis and I was about to regress him back to his first session he suddenly announced that Sidney wanted to talk to me. Feeling some curiosity about what he meant I agreed to listen. My subject began speaking in the brogue of a native Australian, like Paul Hogan as

Crocodile Dundee in the movies, and identified himself as Sidney. Sidney said he had been a general practitioner who had treated the Australian Aborigines in the eighteenth century but was now in spirit working through my client to help him to become a healer. I questioned Sidney about the procedures for correcting the back and chest problems to which he replied that the back pain had been relieved by removing an injured disc from the spine. I said it was my understanding that when a disc is removed the spin has to be fused, therefore causing restriction. He said, "yes, you're right, except for the disc at the very bottom of the spine. In this case, it doesn't matter. The job was very simple". Sidney volunteered other information about himself. He stated that he would be available, through my client, to further his ability as a healer.

After five years, in our follow-up study, the subject reported he had had no further problems with his health and wished more people could experience what he had in regaining his health. After another five years he called me to report his continuing good health and to let me know he was now a minister.

Early in my experience some problems were resolved without determining the emotional cause even though an emotional origin was likely. But what about physical conditions which are the result of injuries sustained in accidents? Can the mental process alone correct a physical injury?

DAMAGED HIP CARTILAGE

The Parks Research and Education project (PREP. Refer to page #25) Case Number 635-R of October, 1979, is about John, a man who had been injured in a motorcycle accident several weeks earlier. Having broken his wrist he had undergone bone graft surgery but his wrist had failed to heal. In addition to the wrist injury John's hip had been damaged and, for this the doctor had advised that an artificial implant would be required within the month.

John was hypnotized and directed to mentally scan the injured area and describe what he observed. He said his hip-bone was chipped and pitted on the edges and there was no cartilage between the hip and the femur bone. This was causing the pain and swelling of his leg. In addition, the bone graft in his wrist had not healed because he was not getting enough blood to the injured area.

I asked him if he thought he could repair the damage. "No" he said, "I can't but Lola can". I asked him who Lola was and he answered that she was a woman who came to him mentally to help with the healing of his wrist and hip. He added that the wrist would heal by stimulating the affected area with natural body heat and increasing nerve activity. I then suggested he could do this by mentally directing heat and nerve activity to the area. He responded that he was doing this and the wrist was healing. He said Lola would evaluate the hip injury and would treat the problem at our next visit. John's leg was swollen twice its normal size, very painful, and he walked with crutches. An appointment was made for the following week.

When John arrived it was apparent that his hip condition had not improved but his wrist had healed. He was again hypnotized and directed to experience the presence of Lola. She immediately appeared in his mind and began the repair of his damaged hip. As she worked John described her actions as, "pulling the leg bone from the hip socket, taking a gray salve from her own hip and placing it on the injured bone and socket". Having done this she replaced the bone in the socket. Lola explained to John the substance would turn white and harden in two days then the repair would be complete. During this process Lola told John to tell me not to worry about her taking the substance from her own hip inasmuch as she had the power to rejuvenate it.

John was asked to return the following week to evaluate his condition and, on his arrival, it was noted that the swelling was completely gone from his leg and he was without his crutches. He said his hip had been sore for about two days following Lola's treatment. The swelling and pain had ceased and he was returning to work. Two years later John reported total recovery was still in effect.

John was present in my class when a lady came with a hip problem. She was planning surgery to have a hip joint replaced. We used John and Lola to evaluate the problem. I hypnotized John and made contact with Lola and she determined there was bone deterioration in the hip joint and nerve stimulation was all that was needed to restore this system. This condition connected to the emotion of resentment for not having the support of her husband in things she wanted to do. Hypnotic suggestion, to increase the nerve activity in the joint and to resolve the negative emotion, was all that was needed. The hip remained functional until her death more than fifteen years later.

CALCIUM BONE SPURES

Evelyn came to my class one night with a foot problem. Her doctor, after taking an x-ray, determined that she had a calcium spur growing off the heel of her right foot. He stated that surgery would be painful and the spur would probably grow back. He suggested using a sponge pad in her shoe to relieve the pain while walking.

Under hypnosis, Evelyn was directed to mentally observe the problem area. She described this spur as being one and a quarter inch long with a quarter inch base tapering to a fine point at the end. I suggested an increase in body heat and nerve stimulation in the area around the spur with the idea that heat would melt the calcium and nerve action would carry away the residue. While this condition was being experienced Evelyn reported intense pain in her foot. Without her knowing what I was doing I then, without touching her, started a stroking action with my hands from her heel to her toes. Evelyn said, "I don't know what you are doing but it feels like you are pulling the pain out the end of my toes". Her mental observation determined that the spur had been shortened by one-half inch. Evelyn found that walking was less painful. She was to return to class the following week.

At the next class it was suggested that her mind would create a chemical in the area of the spur which would, in fact, dissolve it. At this suggestion Evelyn described the sensation of a bubbling effect, like champagne bubbles, starting just below her knee and moving down her leg to the spur. The feeling then became more like a scrubbing action that was dissolving the growth. This, too, caused pain in her foot and I again did the stroking action until the pain ceased. Evelyn determined the spur was shortened by another half inch.

While in class a week later Evelyn mentally determined that the spur was now only a quarter inch long. Considering that the previous methods might affect the foot bone I decided the rest of the spur should be removed by a filing action. I suggested to Evelyn that I would mentally file the remainder of the spur from her foot. Evelyn described the flaking of the spur caused more intense pain than the melting method. Again, the stroking procedure eliminated the pain and the rest of the spur was removed. A few days later Evelyn had her doctor x-ray her foot again and it was confirmed the spur had been completely removed by the hypnotic method.

ng these sessions Evelyn determined that the spur had been formed by the notion of resentment due to her feelings of restriction. She and her husband had purchased a motor home to travel around the country but instead of traveling her husband chose to drive ten miles from home to a fishing hole and, while he fished Evelyn sat in the motor home alone with little to occupy herself. She had resentment of this so, two weeks later, another spur started to form at a different spot on her foot. Through hypnosis another effort was made to get her to resolve the negative emotion, this time successfully, and she had no further problem of this nature.

If you find you can not, or will not, get out of a situation it is necessary for you to change your attitude toward the it.

TUMORS

James, age fourteen, came to my office to have evaluated back pains which he had been experiencing for more than two years. One day at school the pain was so bad he was sent home and then taken to a doctor by his parent. An x-ray showed an abnormal growth on his spine so arrangements were made to have him return for an MRI scan and biopsy. He had been told this procedure would be painful.

It was prior to his return to the doctor James was referred to me by his aunt who thought he might benefit from hypnosis. He responded to this quickly and easily and, during a fifteen-minute hypnotic evaluation, it was determined that at mid-spine there was a growth about an inch in diameter and blue in color. The problem related to two past experiences, one of which connected to a school bully always "being on his back". The other experience happened when he was four years old. I never enquired as to the nature of this experience. When James resolved the negative emotions of these past problems I directed his attention to the growth on his spine. I then suggested we could remove this growth by a mental process. James said in that instant the growth was somehow severed from his spine, bursting into tiny stars that just vanished in a flash. I then suggested that when he returned to the doctor any procedure performed on him would be comfortable and free of pain.

A few weeks later I accompanied James and his family to his doctor's appointment. The doctor was asked about the necessity of a biopsy if the MRI could not locate a problem. He stated that the x-ray had shown there was a problem and they would find what it was. We waited while the doctor, nurse and MRI technician could be heard in the adjoining room discussing the procedure. The technician could not find the problem and suggested the doctor was looking at the wrong location. Then using the original x-ray they went ahead and did a biopsy at the indicated distressed area. Neither the MRI nor the biopsy determined a growth or abnormal condition of the spine.

Following the procedure all the medical personnel present congratulated James for going through the process without expressing that he was in pain. James has had no further back problems for the past nine years.

FEET AND LEG PROBLEMS

In 1987, a 52-year old woman was brought to me in a wheelchair by her husband. She had been treated by a doctor who determined she would never be able to walk again because of the deterioration of the muscles in her legs. During a one-hour session it was determined that the condition related to the emotion of feeling restricted by her husband. Following this session she was able to get out of her wheelchair and walk with a cane. After another session, a few days later, she put away her cane, walked, and ran, without assistance.

One day she called me to report that she had walked proudly into her doctor's office and he remarked, "You're not walking, you are just in a state of hysteria". This incident happened more than twelve years ago and the lady is still walking proudly without assistance.

We tend to list only our successes but we also have our failures. In everyone a belief system is involved. Faith plays a part in success but, most of all, it is the free choice of the individual. Sometimes a person will choose to keep the problem rather than change the situation that is causing it.

One woman in the research project had experienced several heart attacks. Her doctor told her that one more might kill her so she entered our project. She learned the problem related to her attitude toward her husband. When she was made aware of the cause she chose to withdraw from the project stating, "He's going to get his even if it kills me".

MULTIPLE SCLEROSIS

In 1972, I had occasion to work with a man who had Multiple Sclerosis. We determined that the origin and cause of his problem was due to the fact that his wife left him for another man who had been his friend. He fully understood that this experience and the emotion connected with it was the cause of his problem but he simply refused to do anything about resolving the emotion. However, he was impressed enough with the process to recommended it to another MS patient.

This referral was a woman just out of the Mayo Medical Clinic who had been diagnosed with Multiple Sclerosis and had been given fewer than four years to live. She had been told there was no cure for her problem. The only suggested treatment was physical therapy which might or might not, help. She was told her condition would continue to deteriorate until her death.

At our first meeting her husband and their three teen-age children were present. They all agreed she should try my method of hypnotherapy. The case required several sessions because I evaluated each connection of the physical, emotional, and spiritual expressions. I found a connecting link between the taking of a life in a past life experience and that of another in her present existence.

When she became pregnant for the fourth time her family was in a situation where a child would be a problem. The family, and her doctor, all agreed an abortion was the best choice to make. She went through this operation without a problem.

When she became pregnant again her family suggested another abortion. She did not agree with this decision. However, because of her family's insistence, she had another abortion. This time, during recovery, her left arm became numb. The doctor suggested the numbness would go away, but it did not. Instead of improving, the whole left side of her body weakened and took on the condition diagnosed as Multiple Sclerosis. This was her condition when she came to try hypnosis. Medical people were never able to tell her what had caused the problem or where in her body the problem started.

At our final session it was determined the condition occurred in the right rear area of the brain and the energy from the spine could not get past the point of damage. When I asked if this damage could be repaired she replied, "It doesn't have to be repaired: we can find an alternate route".

I then suggested the energy would start at the base of the spine, move up to the damaged area, and then find another route to give energy to the left side of her body. She experienced an energy sensation which moved at a right upper direction in her brain and then diminished. This session was ended with plans to do another evaluation later.

Before another session could be scheduled she and her family moved from the area and I lost contact with them. However about fifteen years later I was relating this case to a class when one of the students spoke up and said, "You're talking about my aunt". I then decided to try and locate the family to update my records.

Through her husband's employer the woman, and her husband, were located and advised of my request to find them. She called me at my office and brought me up to date about her condition. She stated that she had not fully recovered but that her condition had stabilized and she was doing fine. I learned she had returned to college, earned a Family, Child, and Marriage Counseling Degree, and was a practicing Certified Hypnotherapist.

My understanding of Multiple Sclerosis is that it is caused as the result of any emotion which is too intense for the nerve system to handle thereby causing damage to a nerve conductor preventing energy from going beyond the point of damage.

I compare this condition to the source of electrical power which supplies electricity to light our cities. We have a source (generator) which sends energy through wires for a distance until a transformer is needed to send it further along the wires. When too much power reaches this unit it blows up and none can get beyond that point until the transformer is repaired or replaced.

In my evaluation of this woman's condition I learned she had experienced a past life with her present mother. When she was age ten, in this past life, her mother had beaten her to death. In her present life, when she reached age ten, her mother had again beaten her severely. The connection of taking a life (because of the abortions) caused an emotional expression too intense for her nervous system to handle and had damaged a part of the nerve system.

One suggestion for resolving her problem was for her to confront her mother with the information of the past and to establish forgiveness between them. During my association with her she was too frightened of her mother to ever bring about a resolution of her problem. Even though she may have never resolved the conflict with her mother she obviously resolved something within herself to stabilized her condition.

There is no way of knowing how the mind will respond to the direction given during the hypnotherapy process. Many of my most successful cases responded to the question, "can you repair it?" The manner of repair was the choice of the individual and/or was a spontaneous response to the question. I suggest the mind knows the origin and cause of any deficiency and knows its own best way of resolving the problem.

ANEURYSMS

One day, while on police patrol, a city police commissioner joined me as I drove around on my assigned beat. Our conversation eventually turned to hypnotism and the therapy process. The commissioner asked me to stop at his office and talk to his wife who had been feeling poorly for several days and was spending her time resting on a couch there.

I stopped to visit with her a few minutes and then left to continue my patrol alone. Three days later the commissioner called me to ask what I had done to help his wife, as after I left his office, she had got up from the couch to work and had been going strong ever since.

I invited him and his wife, to visit a hypnosis class I was giving. This class was held once a week for three months. Each time they came the commissioner would wait in his car while his wife took part in the class. One night it was too cold and rainy to wait outside so he came into the building. He took a chair to a far corner of the room and sat facing the wall and it was obvious he was afraid of the topics being discussed.

One evening he came to my home and told me he had just learned of an aneurysm in his stomach. He wanted me to do what I do and make it go away. I could see and feel a spot on his stomach which protruded, rising and falling with each beat of his heart. I worked with him making an evaluation as to the origin and cause of his problem. He responded well to the application of hypnosis and in less than fifteen minutes his stomach became calm, no longer pulsating as it had done prior to hypnosis.

On his return to the doctor an examination showed no signs of a problem. His doctor monitored his condition for the next six months at which time he was given a clean bill of health and told he could again play golf and bowl.

Several years later the commissioner called to tell me he had had another physical examination. The x-ray technician asked him if he knew there was an aneurysm in his stomach and told him a sleeve of calcification had formed around the aneurysm to keep it from rupturing. This calcium sleeve had to have been formed in the fifteen minutes it took to evaluate the problem on his visit to my home.

POISON SPIDER BITE

In 1992, I received a phone call from a friend who was at a hospital with her granddaughter who had been bitten by a brown spider. She had waited a week before seeking medical attention. Surgery was necessary in an attempt to save her leg and this required the leg to be cut in four places from the knee to the ankle. Gauze was placed around the arteries to absorb the dead flesh caused by the poison. It had been replaced three times a day for several days without any improvement and the doctors said they might have to amputate her leg.

While her grandmother watched, I hypnotized the girl and directed her through my process of regression therapy. I suggested she could repair the damage to her physical system using her imagination. She pictured using a garden hose to clean the wound by flushing the dead skin away. She used this imaginary process several times the rest of the day and the next morning when the doctor came to replace the gauze, he found the arteries clean and healthy looking. She said the doctor was surprised and confused by the change in her condition. She was released from the hospital the next morning. Only the memory, and the scars on her leg, remains of this incident.

HEART PROBLEMS

In 1983, a friend introduced me to a male member of her family who had experienced a heart attack. He was diagnosed as needing heart by-pass surgery. However, his physical condition was such that surgery could not be performed until his health improved so diet and exercise were recommended. He was hesitant about trying hypnosis but consented after family encouragement.

During the first and only session I had with him it was determined that the fear of fire was connected to his problem. At the age of eighteen months he had been left in the care of his grandmother. She was fixing breakfast when a skillet on the stove caught fire and he observed her scream and grab her chest. When his mother returned his grandmother told her she had almost had a heart attack over the incident. At the age of seven he and a

35

friend were playing with firecrackers and caused a vacant field to catch fire, and during World War ll, he and the crew had to abandon ship after it was bombed and set afire. These incidents each had the emotion of fear with connections to the heart.

While under hypnosis I had him mentally look at the heart area and describe the condition. He said there was a problem with three arteries; Two were clogged with a thick yellow rubbery substance and one was in a black crystallized condition. I suggested an increase in the blood pressure to push this substance through the arteries. He told me this caused the arteries to swell like a balloon so I backed off from this procedure. I then suggested to him that I was using my fingers to massage the arteries in order to break up this yellow substance and allow it to move through them. Actually I was physically moving my fingers in a massaging motion just above his chest with the thought that I was really massaging the arteries. During this procedure he said the substance was actually moving through the two clogged arteries but the black one was beyond repair.

At his next physical examination several weeks later it was determined he was ready for surgery. Following the by-pass surgery he was shown the substance that had been removed from the arteries. He said it was exactly what he had seen in his mind when mentally observing it during the hypnotic process. Nine years later a heart pacemaker was necessary. Early in the year 2000, a phone call with his wife confirmed they were still enjoying life.

REFERENCES

Berheim, H. Suggestive Therapeutics. 1887.
Bramwell, Miles. Hypnotism: Its History, Practice, Theory. 1903.
Hudson, Thomas J. The Divine Pedigree of Man. 1907.
          The Evolution of the Soul. 1904.
          The Law of Mental Medicine. 1903.
          The Law of Psychic Phenomena. 1898.
          A Scientific Demonstration of the Future Life. 1909.
Lee, S. A. The Practice of Suggestion. 1901.
Moll, Albert. The Study of Hypnotism. 1889
Schrenck-Notzing. The Use of Hypnosis in Psychopathia Sexualis. 1895.
Wood, Henry. Ideal Suggestion Through Mental Photography. 1893.

*Note: The above listed books were written between the years 1887 and 1909. This period was known as "The Golden Age of Hypnotism". Most are of foreign origin and were spread around the world during those years. The majority of references to the hypnotic phenomena stem from these origins.

Chapter Four
THOUGHTS ARE THINGS

The words we speak and the words we hear continue to affect us long after they leave our conscious memory. They can lay hidden in the subconscious forming our personality and affecting our actions. If we fully understood the effect of our words and actions towards others we would be more cautious of our expressions.

In my first book, The Inner Mind, and in other sections of this book, I mention experiences I have had in helping others with problems which seemed to resist all other forms of treatment until hypnotism was employed. The most satisfying of my accomplishments are those concerning children.

CHILDREN AND EDUCATION

One day a boy of thirteen was brought to me for help. It had already been established that his problem had to do with the death of his younger brother who had been killed while riding a bicycle. He felt responsible for his brother's death because it had been his bicycle the boy was riding when he was struck by a car.

Following the incident the boy lost interest in everything, his school, hobbies and the people around him. I was told that the school counselors had no success in their efforts to resolve the boy's indifference. A psychiatrist had told his mother that he would prefer not to work with him for fear of creating additional psychological problems. It was this same indifferent attitude that I faced when the boy was brought to me. The family had traveled more than four hundred miles to see me so an effort, on my part, had to be made.

Our session consisted only of inducing the hypnotic attitude and sincerely suggesting to the boy that he had been born into this life for a purpose and that we must all serve our purpose as best we can. (I believe there is a purpose behind every action that extends beyond one's conscious awareness.) I suggested that we are all subject to sad experiences which are a part of life's growing and learning process and I assured him he was not responsible for his brother's death.

About two weeks later the boy's mother called to tell me there had been so much improvement in the child that they wanted to come back for another session. At that visit it took it took less than thirty minutes to repeat the hypnotic suggestions as given before. I noticed the boy no longer sat off by himself looking into space and he joined in the conversation and was proud and excited about his improvement.

Two months later I received a copy of his school report card for the 1969-70, school year with a note attached stating it was at his request that I be given this information. His grades had gone up from a no-credit "F" in the first quarter to an above "C" average in the third quarter. His teacher had also written a note commenting on his change of attitude and the improvement in his schoolwork. I am proud that this fine lad believed in me, and what I had to offer.

This next case involved a boy of eighteen who came when hypnotism was suggested as a last resort to help with his problem. He was still in school, having been placed in a class for the mentally retarded since the age of twelve. School counselors had been unable to find a way to help him and medical doctors couldn't find any physical cause for the boy's inability to learn. He had not been able to pass the written examination for a driver's license on two previous occasions.

Our first visit was to acquaint him with me and to test his response to the process of hypnosis. At a second visit a few days later, I hypnotized him and directed him to recall the first time he had a problem of learning. He recalled an experience at age twelve when he was in the sixth grade. While reading his schoolbook in front of the class his teacher had reprimanded him very severely for the way he was reading. From that moment on he had been unable to concentrate on his lessons.

His parents confirmed this time of change in his schoolwork remembering that he, thereafter, seemed to be looking around as if waiting for something to happen each time he attempted to study. They also confirmed that he had been in the sixth grade when he was placed in the mentally retarded class. After finding the source of his problem suggestions were given to assure him that his teacher had only been trying to help, to teach him rather than having a personal grudge against him for his manner of reading. To help convince him of these suggestions I used a process of guided imagery to create an image of a spiritual entity who came to assure him he could overcome this inner fear and improve his learning ability. In just two weeks the boy had been advanced to the upper classes in school.

He had also taken and passed the test for his driver's license. Three years later, after completing his enlistment in the military service the young man came to thank me. He wanted me to know what a difference those two sessions had made in his life.

SKIN PROBLEMS

A girl of sixteen was brought to me for a skin problem as large welts covered her body from head to foot. Medical diagnosis determined that she had hives and her doctor suggested calcimine lotion as treatment. Under hypnosis she was directed just to relax while I assured her that her body condition would return to normal in a short time. Thirty minutes after her departure from my office she had returned home and she called to say the hives and the discomfort were completely gone and that her body showed no signs that the hives had ever been present.

Another young lady came with a rash all over the top of her head, a condition known as psoriasis. The origin and cause of this problem was connected to her having observed her parents having sex when she was about five years of age. The psoriasis had appeared on her head for the first time when she had her first sexual experience and, on learning the origin and cause of her problem, she was able to resolve it in one session.

PHOBIAS

A young lady came to see if hypnotism could relieve her of the fear of hypodermic injections. She worked in a dental office and was going to have some of her own dental work done, which would require injections which were frightening to her. One session, a few days before her treatment, was all that was necessary. I simply suggested there would be no pain or fear and she would, in fact, find the experience pleasant. She called me a few days later to tell me she had gone through a series of "shots" (hypodermic injections) without any unpleasantness.

WEIGHT & SMOKING

Common requests for assistance with hypnotism are from persons who want to stop smoking or to lose weight. Assisting a person with these problems involves more than just hypnotizing them and suggesting they stop these habits. Subconscious reasons, without correction, will overcome hypnotic suggestions so one must find the origin and cause of the expressions in the subconscious before the condition can be adjusted.

A female nurse tried almost every known method to lose weight without success. She tried hypnosis as a last resort and it was learned that her husband insisted she be heavy and unattractive because he had a physical deformity and feared losing her if she was attractive to other men. Her desire to please her husband was stronger than her desire to lose weight.

VISION PROBLEMS

A man came to Parks Research and Education Project (PREP) with a vision problem. When tested by an optometrist he could not read an eye chart from across the room without his glasses which he had had to wear since age seven. At our first session I determined that the origin and cause of his vision problem related to an incident when he was that age. He and a brother were playing mumblety-peg, a boys' game in which a jack-knife is tossed from a number of positions so that it always lands upright with the blade stuck in the ground in the opponent's marked-off territory. The loser, originally, had to draw a peg from the ground with his teeth.

The man had thrown his knife before his brother was clear in retrieving his own knife and this had struck his brother in the eye. The boy was taken to a hospital, treated and released. No damage had been caused to his brother's sight. However, the emotion of fear over what he may have done to his brother affected his own sight.

While in hypnosis he reviewed this past experience and resolved the connecting negative emotion. A follow-up appointment was made for a week later and on his return he was without his glasses. He said that one of the most pleasant experiences in his life was driving from Riverside to Los Angeles and back and reading the billboards along the roads WITHOUT HIS GLASSES.

BIRTH MISCARRIAGE

At one of my metaphysical classes a young lady talked about not being able to give birth, having already suffered two miscarriages. She worked at a chemical laboratory and thought working around chemicals was causing this inability.

We took a few minutes to do a hypnotic evaluation of the origin and cause of her problem and learned the origin occurred at age five, the cause being a negative emotion about having children. As a child she had observed her parents in a verbal confrontation at which time she said to herself, "If this is the way life is, I'm not going to bring any children into this world". She grew up and married, having no conscious memory of this experience. Early in her marriage she became pregnant twice, miscarrying both times.

I regressed her to the cause of her problem and worked her through the experience to a more positive emotion. She was able to use her imagination to change her thoughts of not wanting to have children.

Apparently she succeeded in making the emotional change for, several years later I met her in a grocery market shopping with two healthy boys. She told me their births had been natural and easy. This was proof to me that she had resolved the emotional cause of the miscarriages in just one fifteen minute hypnotic session.

VERTIGO

According to Webster's Deluxe Dictionary <u>vertigo</u> is a "disordered state in which the individual, or the individual's surroundings, seem to whirl dizzily, or a dizzy, confused state of mind".

In the Parks Research and Education project a lady came to find an answer to a problem of dizziness that would come and go in her life. As we evaluated the problem she regressed to a past life where, as a five-year-old, she had displayed psychic abilities. Because of this psychic expression, the heretics of the community were coming to take her from her father and rid her of this "evil". To prevent her being taken away her father took her into the mountains and threw her into a ravine and while she was falling, she had a spinning sensation and dizziness. On striking the ground she died and entered the spirit world. When I asked her what this experience had to do with the present, she remembered her father, in her present life, had been a road-builder. He had taken his family into the mountains to show them a road he had helped build and while he was holding her baby sister in his arms, he started walking towards the embankment. She thought he was going to throw the baby into the ravine and this association, along with the thought of her past life experience, caused the return of the vertigo.

Following this revelation under hypnosis she has never again experienced the expression of vertigo. Since the age of five, in her present life, she has expressed a psychic ability and has become a very good channel to the spirit world.

SCLERODERMA (SILICONE POISONING) & LUPUS

At the NGH conference in New Hampshire during August, 1993, I worked with a lady who said she had a condition known as Lupus. In June, 1994, she called to say she no longer had that problem but now was suffering with Scleroderma. After a mastectomy she had had silicone implants which had ruptured and silicone poisoning had spread throughout her body resulting in a life threatening condition. She asked me to travel from California to Pennsylvania to help her with this problem.

In a hypnotic regression, lasting over an hour, the following information was given: In 1973, at the age of twenty, she experienced a fibrous breast disease. Tumors started forming in the lymph nodes and breast area about ten years later. These related to the emotions of fear and insecurity following the death of her mother. She said she could not forgive her mother for leaving her. In hypnosis I traced the origin of these emotions to a moment, when she was two years of age, experiencing fear of her mother. By using the ideo-motor technique we connected over four hundred additional experiences to this same emotion.

During this same session she mentally observed pinhead size white spots on her liver in groups of eight. She also found a problem in her left kidney and gall bladder. She had experienced stomach pains ever since the silicone poisoning occurred and I found she had her first stomach problem at age eleven and this revealed the emotion of feeling powerless. She connected over seventy additional experiences to this emotion. Her liver was first offended at age eight and associated to the emotion of the fear of making mistakes. She found two hundred and ten additional experiences to this emotion. Her kidney was first offended also at age eight and tied to the emotion of anger toward injustice. She added over a hundred additional experiences to this emotion.

I started the session by having her reconstruct the past negative experiences to a positive attitude and then do a mental cleansing of each of these organs, one at a time. During this process she experienced tingling sensations throughout her body and felt much better following the session. She continued to improve health-wise and today, in the year 2000, she says she is feeling great. She is a hypnotherapist using my method to help others experience relief from problems where other methods have failed.

MY METHOD OF HYPNOTHERAPY

Before I work with anyone I always ask God, Christ, and my personal guides to assist me in my purpose

KEY PHRASES:

Everything you have ever experienced is recorded and retained in your mind and body systems.

The only thing that interferes with the recovery of past information is your conscious diversion.

It's your mind and body that has all the information about you.

The key to recovering information is to LISTEN.

I am going to have your mind reveal to you_____

THE PROCESS

- IDENTIFY THE ORIGIN OF THE PHYSICAL DEFICIENCY:
- IDENTIFY THE CONNECTING EMOTION:
- DETERMINE THE ORIGIN OF THE EMOTION:
- (This could be currant or past life)

CLEAN HOUSE.

(Direction for reconstruction of the connecting experiences)

You have heard I'm sure, that in times of danger, or an emergency, a persons entire life flashes across their mind. This can and does happen.

I am going to have your mind start from the first experience (Origin of the negative emotion) and come forward an pick out every experience where the negative emotion offended your body in the same manner as the first experience.

As each experience comes into your awareness your mind will look at it, change it, and go on to the next experience until you are all the way up to the present moment. Your mind will do all of this in seconds from now.

By using the ideo-motor process we can determine the number, frequency, and the intensity of the connecting experiences.

SELF-PUNISHMENT

I worked with a woman who, for eight years, had been unable to talk except in a forced, raspy voice. She had been taken to twenty-two doctors and two psychiatrists in California and Mexico without success. As a last resort she agreed to try hypnosis and in two thirty-minute sessions I had her speaking in a clear, beautiful voice.

Under hypnosis she related that, as a ten year old, she teased a woman who couldn't talk. Her mother had warned her not to do this because one day this might happen to her. In later years her mother died and the woman was left with the responsibility for caring for an ill younger brother. This brother had contracted tuberculosis and was confined to a hospital. When he was released to her care she became frightened fearing her own children would contract the disease if her brother had not been cured. She insisted he be re-admitted to the hospital for further treatment.

Following an operation her brother died. She felt responsible for his death as she had forced him back into the hospital. She told herself she would fast as self-punishment for his death. After two weeks of putting off fasting she felt she needed to punish herself in another way and, while thinking of a way to further punish herself, her voice became affected

Several weeks later she called and her voice was again forced and raspy. She had gone to church and the minister had told her she had not been punished enough for her sins.

Embarrassments, disappointments, frustrations, fears, guilt, and other negative emotions of childhood impressions produce emotional scars that remain in the subconscious mind and cause problems later in life. Ideas put into the subconscious mind are the foundation whereby the thought and actions are reflected by the conscious mind. Mental impressions, generally formed in childhood, are the causes of psychic maladjustments that grow with the child and turn out to be the fundamental, or at least contributing, causes of illness, which, on the surface, have no connections with the person's past. In my work I have found that mental and physical deficiencies are the result of negative emotional experiences, which have occurred at the average age of five. Emotional scars can, however, be caused at any age and are dependent upon the individual's mental and physical stability relating to the experience. As for the treatment of the mind in relation to psychosomatic conditions, including physical ailments, it is a fact that no cure ever was, or ever can be, affected by mental processes until the subconscious mind of the individual is impressed with a belief in the effectiveness of the means employed, whether it be in the form of pills, surgery, or hypnosis. With hypnosis, and the process of age regression, it is possible to go directly to the origin and cause of the problem. Every emotional, physical and spiritual deficiency has its origin and cause recorded in the mind systems. Regression therapy can evaluate, improve, and perhaps resolve, any of these expressions, and can do it in minutes.

The fields of medicine and psychology require special education. Hypnotism can certainly be a tool to these professions. However, hypnotism is also a special field of its own. To be effective in the professions of Hypnotism and Mesmerism requires specialized skills and knowledge as would any other profession and, is indeed, a separate and independent service.

Being educated in another profession does not make a person an authority on hypnotism, or qualified in its uses. There are even experts, authorities, and knowledgeable persons, who are by no means infallible in their own fields. I have no doubt that it was my sincerity, belief, and purpose that have made my work in hypnosis possible for me where others have failed. Aside from my knowledge of the mechanism of hypnotism I think the element of "privilege" had the most bearing on the results and accomplishments of my use of this science.

"Mechanism" means the process, methods, and techniques of hypnotism. "Privilege" is a term used by those in the spiritual realm for those who have earned the right to higher knowledge, i.e. Talking to God and other spirit entities.

Chapter Five
REGRESSION THERAPY AND HOW IT WORKS

The process of regression therapy is based on the premise that everything the individual has ever experienced is recorded and retained in the mind systems. The mind appears to have multi-levels of consciousness, which we make up into three main systems and identify as the conscious, subconscious, and super-conscious. Your conscious mind is *what you do*. Your subconscious mind is *what you are*. Your super-conscious mind is *the Soul, Spirit, or God element*. These three mind systems function independently of each other simultaneously. They each do their job alone and, as a unit. It appears the best attitude an individual can have is when these three levels of consciousness are thinking and acting alike, recognizing the super-conscious as the strongest.

It is easier and more effective to reach the subconscious and super-conscious systems when the conscious system is inactive. Therefore, the process of hypnosis is to quiet the conscious system thereby enhancing the communication and response of the other systems.

Experience is absolute and circumstances, and their effect upon the individual, is self-contained within the confines (consciousness) of that individual. Any past experience is there for the asking if not restricted by conscious diversion.

Everything we experience contains emotions, positive or negative. The stronger the emotion the more it affects the physical systems. Love and fear are the two basic emotions. Love always affects the physical systems in a positive way while fear is basic to the negative emotions of anger, guilt, resentment, hate, and other negative expressions, all of which offend the physical systems.

Hypnotic regression shows that these emotions, as well as a personality, are present at birth. Reinforcement and/or change of the personality and emotions occur with conscious experience to become subconscious imprints in the new physical system. Most emotions are re-experienced and/or reinforced by the average age of five. It appears that once a negative emotion is expressed enough to imprint the subconscious it becomes the basic cause of the physical deficiencies that occur later in life. The extent of these physical deficiencies are compatible to the intensity and/or accumulation of the emotion. Even though these negative emotional imprints can cause physical deficiencies at any time following an experience there appears to be an average of ten years from the first emotional imprint before the physical systems are severely damaged.

PHYSICAL-EMOTIONAL CONNECTIONS

These are my observations of the body/mind connections.

PROBLEM	EMOTION
Headaches & Migraines	Anger
Eyes & Ears	Did not want to See/Hear___
Mouth & Throat	Communication (Saying or Not saying)
Hands & Arms	Resentment about Giving or taking
Shoulders & Neck	Resentment. responsibility or work load
Chest & Breast	Fear and Insecurity
Heart	Lack of love and/or affection
Stomach	Worry
Hips and Back	Resentment
Feet & Lower Leg	Restrictions
Knees & Upper Leg	Lack of Support
Reproduction Systems (Involving Sexual Expressions)	Fear, Guilt, Shame
Diabetes	Rejection
Emotional Cancers	Rage
Herpes & Aids	Sexual Betrayal
Psoriasis	Sexual Shame and/or Guilt
Multiple Sclerosis	Any emotion too intense for nervous system
Right side of body	Emotion directed toward a male
Left side of body	Emotion directed toward a female
Centered in the body	Situation – No Gender Involved

Every negative emotion, if not resolved within a reasonable period of time, will damage the physical systems that relate to the connecting emotion. Every physical disorder is connected to a negative emotion or combination of emotions. The stress factor or intensity of the emotion determines the amount of damage to the physical system. Other physical disorders all have connections to negative emotional experiences.

As long as these negative emotions are present the physical systems are being restricted from their normal functions. By resolving the negative emotions through the process of hypnosis the deficiencies of the physical systems can be improved or corrected. I have yet to find a physical deficiency that did not connect to an emotional cause when the evaluation was made through the process of regression therapy.

Take a moment now and look at yourself, and others. To how many of the above physical and emotional connections can you relate?

THE PROCESS

The process for recovery of the offended systems is to first determine the origin of the physical offense and identify the connecting emotion. The next step is to determine the origin of this emotion and when accomplished the individual is directed to re-live the experience and, while so doing, recognize that there was an instant of choice in relating to the experience by either a positive, negative, or indifferent response. The subject is then directed to use his/her imagination and reconstruct the experience with a positive or indifferent emotion. When the original negative emotional imprint is changed all of the following experiences that have connected to the original negative emotion also have to be changed. This is done by using the imagination to create a different reality to the experience at the subconscious level of that particular experience.

The idea that a person's entire life can flash across his mind in seconds is very real, it can and does happen. With hypnosis this phenomenon can be controlled so that past experiences can be recalled, re-evaluated, and reconstructed in a matter of seconds. On the average, ten to twelve previous experiences can be located, looked at, and reconstructed in thirty to forty-five seconds. If this reconstruction is properly done the negative emotion will no longer be offensive to the physical system, which can then recover.

The mind stores information similar to that of a tape recorder, which records a sequence of events in the exact manner they are received through the microphone. When a tape is replayed, it plays back exactly what was recorded. The mind also records a sequence of events, which we call experiences and when we recall a previous experience the mind can play it exactly as it was recorded, including the emotions. If something is recorded on the tape that is not wanted, or is in some way offensive, adding a change at the end of the recording cannot alter it. The unwanted material has to be erased or taped over. The mind works the same way. If something has been recorded in the mind that is offensive to the physical systems trying to add a different attitude or emotion to the end of the conscious experience cannot change it. The change has to be made at the point it was originally recorded and stored in the subconscious. In making these evaluations the individual is made aware of the instant of choice and a better, more positive, way to respond to the experience is then possible.

Talking about past experiences takes time. Talking also allows the individual to get caught up in the emotion of the experiences. Therefore, I do not have my subjects talk about the past connecting negative experiences. Communication is established by using the ideo-motor technique. Prior to the induction the subject is given the choice to select any finger to represent a yes answer and another finger to represent a no answer. The ideo-motor response, or the movement of the finger, is there even if the subject is unaware of the response. Therefore, the individual is not required to talk about personal and private details of any past experience. By using the ideo-motor process we save time and diminish the emotions connected with the past experience. The ideo-motor process can also identify the number, the frequency, and the intensity of connecting experiences to the original imprint.

I'm amazed by what the mind can do when allowed to determine its own manner of recovery. As hypnotheraptists we need to allow the clients' mind to make decisions as to its own best method of resolving any physical or emotional problem. Only a few years into my practice, I realized the mind was able to determine the method of recovery far better than I was. On several occasions while teaching classes on hypnotherapy, I have worked with clients who chose not to tell me what the actual physical or emotional problem was before I worked with them. During the session I would refer to "the problem" or "the emotion". As long at the client knows what problem they are working on the process seems to work as well. For this reason I find it unnecessary to take medical histories or complete long intake forms. It is my role, as a Hypnotherapist, to be the guide and allow the client to find his/her own best answers.

Working with these concepts we can access the mind and body systems to determine, in just a few minutes, the origin and cause of any deficiency of the physical, emotional, and spiritual expressions.

BRAIN SYSTEMS

In 1990, I discovered that the brain has different areas for the expression of positive and negative thoughts. There is also an area where addiction occurs. While under hypnosis the subject is directed to identify the location and conditions areas and this is done without the subject having any prior knowledge about these systems. Identification is confirmed by an ideo-motor response. The mind will not only identify the location and condition of these systems but cleanse and adjust any offense that may be present. When this mental cleansing occurs there is a flushing, draining, or suction sensation experienced by the subject and when the process is completed the subject confirms the cleansing by an ideo-motor response. Many subjects have reported a relaxed and contented attitude after this cleansing process.

The positive, negative, and addiction systems are located in the same brain area based on whether the subject is naturally right handed, left handed, or ambidextrous. The person who displays ambidextrous traits is generally one who was born left handed and through habit has developed right hand predominance. The right handed person finds the positive system on the right front side of the brain, the negative system at the left rear, and the addiction at the top front center. The left handed person finds the positive system on the brain's left front side, the negative at the right rear, and the addiction at the top rear center. The ambidextrous person may reverse the negative and addiction systems or find the addiction system at the top center of the brain.

Once the subject has experienced the awareness of these brain systems it is easier for him to accept his mind's ability to mentally look at the bones, muscles, nerves, organs, and cells of the body. In this mental observation the nature of the offense to a particular system can be determined. The mind can observe the body systems as they are or as they were at any time in the past. When the subject has made the comparison between the correct condition and the offensive one he/she is directed to mentally correct any damage to the system be it cleansing, adjustment, or repair. Some of my most impressive physical recoveries have been the result of simply asking the mind "Can you repair it?"

Freedom of choice is always involved. The individual can choose to keep the offending emotions, and the physical deficiency, rather than change the emotion. Some do make this choice. Some of the benefits of resisting change are the desire for control, revenge, financial security, emotional security, attention, and security of the familiarity with the present state. Suffering (believing that punishment is deserved) is also a resistant benefit. When there is no change in thought habits there is no change in the condition. When individuals change their thought patterns then it also changes their personality.

I do not want to give the impression that hypnosis and age regression are cure-all methods. In many cases the problem has deteriorated beyond the ability, or the desire, of the individual to recover. Again this is freedom of choice and/or purpose. However, we never know when, or how, it may help until we try.

I am reminded of a statement made by Dr. V. G. Crookshank in the year 1920. In his book Healing Without Medicine, Dr. Crookshank is quoted as saying, "The only satisfactory method of curing illness is to uncover the repressed frustrations of fears, grief's, hatreds, and loves to try to help the person come to terms with himself and divert his energies to more positive and appropriate channels".

The subconscious mind is the source of dreams. Freud explained dreams as a way the sleeping mind fulfills the dreamer's unexpressed wishes and desires. Other psychologists explain dreams as attempts at solving problems. Many people believe dreams are of divine origin symbolizing events predestined as the result of one's purpose in life. Dreams may also be caused by physical sensations. If a person is cold while sleeping he may dream of being in a snowstorm. A person falling from the bed while sleeping may, in that instant, dream he is falling from the top of a high building or other tall structure.

The following is an example of a dream resulting from a childhood emotional experience, which in turn, caused a physical reaction. Whenever the physical reaction occurred in sleep it related to the re-occurrence of the dream.

A boy was brought to me with a bed-wetting problem. He was fourteen years old and had been wetting his bed since the age of nine but he had no awareness of this occurrence until awakening. By hypnotic regression we learned that at age nine his older brother threatened to kill him with a 22-caliber rifle. His brother chased him until he was able to run inside his home and hide. That night he dreamed his brother was again chasing him and during this pursuit, his brother changed into a "bunch of little green men with hatchets" who were threatening to kill him. This dream was revealed while in hypnosis. The boy recalled that each time he wet his bed he had dreamed of being chased by the little green men with hatchets.

The bed-wetting was also aggravated by other emotional conditions in his home. In order to correct the problem I placed the boy in hypnosis and had him recall this dream. When the little green men appeared to him, he said, "There they are". I told him "hold it, don't do anything" as I did not want him to urinate on my couch. He stated that the little green men had stopped but were waving their hatchets, indicating they were going to get him. I encouraged him to stand up to them and not be afraid. He said that when he stopped running and turned on them, they stopped chasing him. I suggested he go after them and chase them away. He did so and they stood off at a distance waving their hatchets and warned him that if he didn't stop chasing them they would sneak back later and get him. I said if he could chase them away then and there, he could do it anytime, and he should, therefore, have no fear of them. With additional assurance the boy chased the little green men until they were out of sight. I followed up this procedure with my technique of making my subject aware of the spiritual power and guidance within himself. His mother reported later that the boy was no longer troubled with his disturbing sleeping habits and his bad dreams were completely gone.

The mind, in its response to hypnotic regression, will express an awareness that appears to have its origin prior to birth. The concept of reincarnation is present in the mind regardless of the belief in it. Religion, sex, age and nationality, make no difference. An individual will sometimes relate to an experience, which appears to have occurred in a prior lifetime. The emotion of the past experience was so strongly impressed it carried over with the spirit into the new body to become offensive to the same physical system that was originally offended.

There are some who practice regression therapy who believe that all present physical and emotional problems are connected to past life experiences. There is no denying that all past life experiences have their link to the present. I have found, however, that mental and physical problems, which are present at birth amount to less than 10% of all problems. These may be connected to a past life experience or may have their origins between the moment of conception and birth.

In the mind there is an unbroken awareness from one's spiritual creation to the present. These prior lifetimes may involve a few, or many, past life experiences and include the time and realm between them. It is the mind's ability to record and retain all that is past, and it is this phenomenon that makes it possible to determine the origin and cause of any physical or emotional problem. The mind has total knowledge of the structure and conditions of the physical body. Not only does it know the origin and cause of a physical or emotional deficiency it knows its own best way to correct these conditions. The mind can also determine the period of time it will take to resolve the problem if the emotional adjustment is made. The solution to many physical and emotional problems is brought about by spirit entities. The success of this method of healing has nothing to do with one's belief in spirit communication. Spirit assistance in healing the ills of the mind and body is probably the most natural and effective method known to man.

Regardless of the application and the use of hypnosis it should be left to those who are properly trained in hypnotism. It may be a tool for other professions but when used by those not thoroughly trained in its process it can be very ineffective.

Chapter Six
HYPNOSIS AND PSYCHIC EXPERIENCES

From all the races and peoples of the earth, and from all times, there have been handed down to us historical and so-called miraculous or supernatural stories and happenings which we have classified as extraordinary, extrasensory, extremely unusual, beyond our natural physical processes, psychic, or even unbelievable.

The usual course is not to admit these phenomena as being authentic and real or to reject them as spurious or imaginary, or to submit the stories to the most rigorous criticism without making a definite judgment in regard to their veracity. It has, however, been accepted that all psychic manifestations of the human intellect, whether designated by the names of spiritualism, mesmerism, hypnotism, miracles, genius, or insanity, are in some way related.

Spiritual mediums, clairvoyants, psychic healers, and hypnotists are becoming better understood although hypnotists are not favored or considered as important in the psychic field. Despite this, the fact remains that clairvoyants, psychics, and spiritual healers assume a hypnotic attitude before expressing their abilities. There are unlimited numbers of writings concerning the phenomena of premonitions, ghost apparitions, telepathy, telekinesis, materialization, and discarnate communication through trance medium ship.

During my forty plus years of experience and investigation into the science of hypnotic regression I have found the following patterns.

The mind is most amazing in its phenomena of memory. After the proper hypnotic attitude is obtained the mind, by direction, can recall any moment of the past and, as such, can determine the instant of changes in the mental and physical attitudes. It is by this method that we are able to correct emotional and physical disorders and bad habits, which have been caused by a prior negative mental attitude. The pattern further discloses that a mental link exists between our physical existence and a spiritual origin and destination, and there are laws that govern the process of one's Soul to an ultimate goal. There are those who have, by their own experiences, accepted the belief in the communication between the living and the dead. Thousands of testimonials have been written to the fact that this type of communication is a regular occurrence to people all over the world. However, the question remains, do these things really happen or is it just a state of mind?

Through hypnotism we can create, in the mind of our subjects, the awareness that they are in direct communication with someone who is deceased, is it a friend, relative, or someone unknown to the subject. From outside observation it appears that this awareness is simply an illusion or hallucination but to the person experiencing this type of communication the awareness is real. This type of expression will sometimes bring the most surprising results.

A few years ago a man was referred to me because of his problem with alcohol. During our interview he explained that he had started drinking excessively following a separation from his wife. He had married a woman with two teen-aged sons from a previous marriage. She had raised her boys to be pacifists and expected them to avoid military service. Being partial to the military, this man talked the older of the two boys into enlisting in the United States Air Force and he was subsequently sent to an overseas base for duty. Shortly after his arrival in the war zone his mother was informed by the military that her son had died of a heart attack. Grieving his death she blamed her husband for his part in encouraging the boy to enlist and their separation was the result. It was only a matter of time before the man took to alcohol to escape his problems. He could not accept the fact that the boy had died of a heart attack so he started investigating, through friends in the service, as to the real cause. He felt that another person had killed the boy.

It was at our second session that I decided to produce an illusion of the boy in the mind of this man and have him question him (the illusion) about his death. This mental communication between the man and the illusion of the boy was done without any verbal report to me. It was confirmed that the young man had appeared in his mind and that the communication was established. After setting this scene I waited.

In the state of hypnosis the physical senses can be altered to different degrees of function. The subject can be caused to see things that are not there or not see things that are there. The hearing, tasting, and feeling senses can be changed likewise.

During this mental communication my subject suddenly spoke out loud the words, "Refrigeration Gas". I interrupted and asked the meaning of his reaction. He replied that his stepson was telling him he had died from being overcome by gases while working on some refrigeration units in a warehouse where he was stationed. At this point my subject stated, "He wants to know who I am talking to". After a pause he said, "I told him about you and how you are trying to help me". I let him communicate with the boy a while longer before I awakened him and questioned him about the experience.

When I asked if he really thought he was talking to his stepson he said, "No one can ever convince me that I wasn't talking to him". The boy told him to tell his mother not to worry, that he was just fine and had actually died from inhaling gas from the refrigeration units. He told his stepson of the separation and that he would not be able to relay this information to his mother. The boy suggested I would also be able to help him with reconciliation.

Clearly this experience as given has no real claim to being a psychic experience. It was strange, however, when it was later learned from the military that the boy had, in fact, been assigned to work on refrigeration. His family had not previously known this fact. A few months later I returned home to find a note on my door from the boy's mother. This note said she had reconciled with her husband and wanted to talk to me about some problems with her younger son. Unfortunately, she lived in a distant city and the meeting never occurred.

Hypnosis also has an association with premonitions and dreams. The following is an example of how hypnotism was used to fill in forgotten pieces to an experience of premonition.

Mr. X was an observer at one of my hypnosis classes and following the activities of the evening requested an opportunity to experience hypnosis. He said he had served with the United States Marines in Korea and explained that while on guard duty an inner voice told him he was going to be shot. He was being given a choice of where he would prefer the shot to strike him. He answered to himself that if he had to be shot he would prefer it to be in his right leg. Three days later he was again on guard duty, walking his post, when he was struck in the right leg by an enemy bullet. He was flown to a hospital in Japan for treatment and amputation of his leg. Following surgery he had no memory of what had taken place for the next eleven days. He believed he had been in a coma. I hypnotized and regressed him to a time the week before the shooting incident and brought him forward, having him relive each day until the lost days were accounted for. He remembered the premonition and of being shot. He recalled being flown to Japan and having his leg amputated and coming down with pneumonia following the operation. He remembered being in an isolated room with a tent-like cover over his bed. He was able to see doctors and nurses coming into his room and talking together without his being able to hear a word or sound from them. He had been in the isolation tent for a period of eleven days, the period of time he had been unable to remember before being hypnotized.

In 1942, I was working for the government as a civilian chief dispatcher of transportation and there were several male and female vehicle drivers working in my division. One of the females was a gypsy, or so we thought. She told fortunes by reading cards, palms, tea leaves, and who knows what else.

One day during a work break she read for me. She told me I would have three children in my life, one boy and two girls and said I would lose one of the girls at birth. She told me I would be going across the ocean and other things that had no real meaning to me. The statement about my children seemed most impressive and stayed with me, somewhat over the years. At the time of the reading I already had a two-year-old son.

In 1943, I joined the Navy and went off to war. Spending the next two years in the South Pacific aboard the aircraft carrier Intrepid. When I returned home in December of 1945, I returned to work at an Air Force base.

In October 1946, my wife was in the final hours of her pregnancy. One morning while sleeping I dreamed a black widow spider was crawling up my right arm and, as I flung my arm so as to shake off the spider struck my wife across her stomach, not hurting her but startling her from her sleep. Within an hour we were at the hospital preparing for the birth of our second child. After my wife was prepared and taken into the delivery room all signs of delivery stopped. She was returned to her room and after two days was sent home.

Exactly one week to the day and hour I had an identical dream of the spider crawling on my arm and, flinging my arm, I again struck my wife across her stomach. We rushed to the hospital and within an hour she gave birth to a perfectly formed beautiful baby girl.

Following the delivery the doctor reported there had been a problem with the birth. He said the umbilical cord had become wrapped around the baby's leg creating a lack of oxygen that caused the heart to swell. He said the condition was such that the baby would not live beyond the age of twelve if she lived at all. The baby died after three days in an incubator.

In July, 1948, our second girl was born. In 1949, my wife had to have a hysterectomy. What was so unusual was the connection between the gypsy's prediction and the birth of our first daughter. This portion of the prediction by the gypsy took six years to complete.

In Chapter One mention was made of some concepts of hypnotic regression and how a person in this condition will often describe experiences of a past life, including an existence between lives. In my first book, <u>The Inner Mind</u>, reference was made to Dick Marsh who regressed to five different past lives. He described himself as "Jose", a fourteen-year-old son of a cobbler in a place called "Cellos" in Ancient Greece, in 680 BC. In the year 1101, at the age of twenty-four, he was called J.B., a bandit in Thrice, a town in the mountains of Spain. In 1650, he was Andrea Galecuis, age thirty-four, a stone-mason in Venice, Italy, and In 1837, he was John Holt, a thirty-six-year-old barrister in Gloucester, England. But what, at that time, was even more amazing was his description of an existence in a spiritual realm between these lives.

In December of 1965, I held a special regression for the purpose of obtaining all the information I could about his life in England in 1837. John Holt said he had been born in the year 1801. At age seven against his wishes his parents forced him to attend the Church of England. He never married because his sweetheart had been run over and killed by a horse and carriage. He died at the age of fifty-two of a heart problem, having been treated for the condition by a friend, Dr. Taylor. At the time of this regression he lived on Clieston Street in Gloucester, England. My subject carefully spelled out the name <u>Clieston</u>. He described Gloucester as being "a day's ride from South Hampton to the southeast". I examined maps of England to locate these two cities and figured it could be called "a day's ride" in light of the mode of transportation related to that era, one hundred and twenty years ago. He added that his father had been a county recorder in the City of Hempstead for some thirty-five years. History revealed, at a later date, that a County Recorder was considered as most honorable in those days in England. John Holt said that prior to 1837, there were no public records concerning births, marriages or deaths as the Church of England kept these records prior to that date.

I had another reason for getting as much information as I could from this regression. A friend, Jeannette Y. Glenn, an astrologer and a writer for several leading astrological magazines, wanted to compare material from a hypnotic regression with information compiled from an astrological reading on the same person, both on his present life and on the most recent past life.* This would be done without either of us knowing the contents of the others material. A story of this experiment, written by Mrs. Glenn, was published in <u>Psychic Review</u> in April of 1973. The story was entitled "The Search for John Holt Into the Fourth Dimension".

To our knowledge an experiment of this nature had never before been done, because of certain attitudes between the astrologers and hypnotists wanting to keep their professions "clean". In 1965, the attitudes about hypnotism were not the best and astrologers were trying to establish themselves as legitimate professionals in their own field.

Mrs. Glenn explained the astrological part of the experiment as being based on the horoscope of my subject. The twelfth-house delineation of the horoscope is an actual map of the immediate last life, because it represents that with which the individual comes into this life. It could also depend on what they have become and the essence of what they are, as far as one may determine such a complex matter.

The astrological contents revealed that the subject was in the legal profession in his last life and was from a most respected background or family line. He was considered to be well off for whatever era he had lived in this most recent incarnation. His horoscope also revealed that he must have lived a normal life span for that period although there were no aspects for marriage indicated in the past. The fact that he was forced into religion in this past life showed a connection to his being an agnostic in his present life.

Mrs. Glenn explained that an incoming ego might often choose to incarnate for a specific purpose, such as this sorrowful karma. He may easily have wasted his life in prison for principles that the past world was not idealistically ready to incorporate. Whatever and however it took place in the past life must certainly be resolved now and blended with the realism the realism of Capricorn or he must starve in a garret in an unfeeling world.

Believing that we had enough facts for verification of the regression information, Mrs. Glenn prepared and sent a letter to the Rt. Hon. Lord Mayor of London, England.

With the experiment up in the air, awaiting a reply from England, Mrs. Glenn again studied the horoscope of my subject. There was no doubt about it; the legal profession had been his background in the past life. With the sun sign of Capricorn, intercepted in the first house, a carry-over from the past should have been a true Capricorn incoming soul, but he had this heavy psychic twelfth-house to clear up before he could go further in his own soul growth. How? The way was clear, with psychic Neptune in trine aspect to energy Mars in Sagittarius from his eighth house, and a testimony to contact with the "Dead" on the astral plane of consciousness.

With six planets in Cadent houses, Dick's abilities would most naturally come to light through a third person or agent, in this case the hypnotist, and make contact with a former life pattern. We could not prove if in fact he was, in reality, in contact with a former life. His chart would most certainly indicate mediumistic potentials by some entity seeking to establish at least, "life after death".

(For those who do not understand the astrological terminology, it may suffice to say that astrological information was very compatible with my regression material.)

In reply to her letter we received the following information from the General Register Office, Somerset House, London, W.C.2.

Dear Madam:
Before 1st, July, 1837, the principal provision for recording births and baptisms, marriages, and deaths or burials, was by means of parish registers kept by clergymen of the Church of England. And any application respecting such records should be made to the officiating minister of the church at which the rite took place. Such records are not deposited here. Records formerly kept by religious denominations other than Church of England are now in the custody of the Record Keeper, Public Record Office, Chancery Lane London, W.C.2. to whom all inquiries should be addressed.

We were unable to communicate with the local Church of England at Hempstead and, to this day, have not been able to verify the existence of John Holt.

Mrs. Glenn said, "Of all the subjects who follow Dick will always stand out in my memory as the most spirited of them all, certainly the most daring and sincere of effort. He said that during his period of time in England he had talked with friends about metaphysical concepts but that his knowledge was limited due to the attitude of the general public about the subject. I got the impression that his nature, or personality, was not unlike that of Dick Marsh today".

Note *JEANNETTE YVONNE GLENN

Raised in San Francisco, California, Jeannette Yvonne Glenn was a concert harpist at the age of nine. She studied astrology under Norma Hammond, president of the California Astrological Society, and joined this group in 1936. Graduation from Berkeley Teacher's College was followed by extensive post-graduate work in psychology. She has served on the personal staff of <u>American Astrology</u> magazine. She is editor of <u>The Astrological Newsletter,</u> a monthly news publication and she is Astrological Technical Advisor to Clark and Associates of North Hollywood for their forecasting programs. Mrs. Glenn has written many articles for astrological magazines and practiced astrology at the professional level for twenty-four years. As of 1967, she was residing with her family in the Costa Mesa-Newport Beach area of

Chapter Seven
A SECOND LOOK

This chapter is a review of the material in Book One of <u>The Inner Mind</u>, which I completed in 1965. Every prediction or event listed in the book did happen. This chapter is meant to be the foundation for the story being told in the subsequent chapters.

On August 7th, 1963, officers of the San Bernardino County Sheriff's Department and officials of the Long Beach and Los Angeles law enforcement agencies took Mr. Hugh McLeod Pheaster into the San Bernardino mountains near Big Bear California to search for the remains of Mrs. Dolores Mae Siddall, whom Pheaster had killed during an abortion attempt. He had dumped her body over an embankment near the highway in that area. Following a two-day-long unsuccessful search Pheaster was returned to Long Beach, California, where the crime had been committed. Following a trial, he was found guilty, sentenced, and incarcerated in a federal prison. Pheaster had been unable to remember the exact location of the body.

At the time of this incident I had been with the San Bernardino City Police Department for eight years, seven of which had also been spent in the research and practice of hypnotism. After learning that Pheaster had been unable to remember the location of the woman's body I went to the Sheriff's Department and offered my services as a hypnotist to try to help Pheaster remember. The authorities, Pheaster, and his attorney agreed to this plan. However, since Pheaster was a federal prisoner, permission for his return to San Bernardino had to be obtained from Mr. James V. Bennett, head of the federal prisons in Washington, D.C. Early in September, 1963, I received word from the Long Beach Police Department that permission had been refused by Mr. Bennett. Sergeant Frank P. Welch, of the Long Beach Police Department, said that Bennett feared possible after-effects of hypnosis on Pheaster and other federal authorities feared hypnosis might make Pheaster "hard to handle" while in federal prison. Hypnotism was not a common practice at that time so it was not surprising when the federal authorities denied our request.

Ironically, hypnosis has, and is now being used with great success by prison psychiatrists in rehabilitating prisoners and making them "easier to handle". It involves no dangers, nor are there ever any after-effects when applied by an experienced, competent hypnotist. It has been proven that hypnosis usually succeeds where everything else fails when working with mentally disturbed people, juvenile delinquents, alcoholics, narcotic cases, and many others.

With the help of hypnotism certain people can express outstanding abilities in the psychic fields. Clairvoyance, telepathy, psychometry, and many other psychic forces can be brought from a dormant condition to a very active expression by the use of hypnosis. It was my privilege to find such a gifted person in Irene, a girl seventeen years of age when her mother had brought her to a class at my office. During the hypnotic process I suggested to her that she might be of help in locating the body of Mrs. Siddall through her sensitivity with psychometry.

Three days later the girl's mother called to report that Irene had dreamed of walking in the mountains and had tripped over the body of a woman. She described the dream, giving a description of the body's size, age, hair color, and clothing. She described the area near and around the body where a tree had been struck by lightning and had broken off at the top. There were piles of rocks and tree stumps nearby. I took this information to the Sheriff's Department and, on checking the record, found that the description of Pheaster's victim and the woman in Irene's dream were identical.

Accompanied by several people I took Irene and her mother to the mountains to search for the remains of the missing woman. I hypnotized her at several different locations along the road before her actions indicated that some force was attracting her over an embankment. She pointed to a spot down the mountainside and attempted to walk over the embankment in the direction she was pointing. A member of our party went down the mountain about twenty-five yards but could find nothing to indicate that the body was at this location. Because of time and weather conditions we had to return to town to wait for another chance to continue the search. As it turned out, it was several months before an opportunity again presented itself.

In March of 1964, the young lady's mother called me to report that Irene had developed a feeling of concern about the missing woman. She indicated a desire to return to the mountains in an attempt to find her. She said Irene kept hearing the woman calling to come and find her. As soon as possible, we returned to the previous location.

Irene was hypnotized and I asked her for directions. She indicated that we would have to go down the mountainside about a hundred yards from the road. Following directions, we were led to an area that was identical to the description given in her dream. A burned tree broken off at the top, tree stumps, boulders, and other points of identification matched the dream. At one particular spot Irene, while under hypnosis, became frightened and pointed to the base of a large manzanita bush and cried, "She's there, She's there". When awakened from hypnosis she showed no fear or concern over the spot she identified as the location of the woman's body. Our search was hampered by the lack of safety equipment since the location was very steep and slippery. I tied a large bandanna to the tree to mark the spot and we returned home for the necessary equipment to continue the search.

Irene's mother suggested we try a regression to see if this method would offer further information about finding the body. In regression, when we take a person to a place and time away from his present lifetime, we always have a change in identity, a different name, a different area of existence and, in most cases, a change in nationality. From all appearances there seems to be a different person altogether. This connection will be discussed as we continue.

On June 17, 1964, Irene experienced her first age regression. It was suggested that her mind would take her back to a time just before being born into her present life. At this point she identified herself as Rebecca.

Rebecca said she felt the woman we were looking for was in the beyond, she needed help and that people on earth, and others, could supply this help with time and work. She felt I was very close to finding the woman as I had gone into the search more deeply than anyone. The woman had asked Irene to come and find her; she wanted her body to be found so we should keep trying.

Rebecca then excused herself, saying her Leader wished to talk to her. She requested that I visit with her again. This closed my first regression with Irene. The instant Rebecca departed Irene's body seemed to become empty of all life and her features became set as in death. I suggested she, Irene, return to the present and the expression of life returned to her body. Never, in the many times I hypnotized this girl, did she remember what had taken place in hypnosis. She had no conscious memory of what had happened or what Rebecca had said. Her only knowledge of her hypnosis was much later when she had an occasion to hear a portion of a taped regression of herself. She could never understand how she was able to talk of so many things with so much conviction.

In our second regression on June 24, 1964, Rebecca confirmed that we were close to finding the body and she would help all she could. She had talked to her Leader about this and he approved of my work. He said I should have more faith and confidence, that maybe next time I visited Rebecca I could talk with him.

It was not until July 13, that I was able to do another regression with Irene. Rebecca again said that we were very close to finding the body and to keep trying. She said it would take patience and a good attitude and it would take longer, even though I was near, because it was not meant for her to be found yet. Rebecca commented that the Leader was very busy but I would get to talk to Him sometime. She would contact me, through Irene, when she had word that I could talk with her Leader.

Rebecca was the one who made contact for our visit on October 6, 1964. In the early afternoon Irene called her mother at work to tell her of a strange experience she had had at school. A complete stranger came up behind her in the hallway, touched her shoulder and said, "Irene?" When she turned around, the boy said, "You are wanted up at Al's tonight". She asked him how he knew she was wanted there and he told her that another boy had asked him to tell the girl with the yellow ribbon in her hair that she was wanted at Al's house tonight. When he turned to point to the other boy he was gone. When Irene turned back the boy with whom she had been talking was also gone. In an instant she was left standing alone in the hallway.

Upon arriving home from school Irene and her mother made plans for us to get together that evening. When they arrived and the regression started we had a strange and exciting experience. Rebecca said she had arranged this contact to advise me she had been assigned a mission and would be gone from time to time. If I attempted to contact her and was not able to do so it would be because she was away on part of this mission. She indicated she would be gone for the next ten to twelve days. I waited only five days and attempted a regression with Irene to see if contact could be made with Rebecca before the time she said she would return. Irene regressed back through her life to the first day of her birth giving, without hesitation, the information I requested at her different ages and when I attempted to take her beyond birth she did not respond. Her body again gave the appearance of an empty shell, as in death, and she would not respond to my direction so she was directed to return to the present moment and awakened.

When contact was again made on October 19, Rebecca was just leaving on another phase of her mission but would spare me a few minutes if I wanted to talk. She had contacted the missing woman two levels below her while on the first part of her mission. The woman was very disturbed, and said that now she did not want to be found. At first she wanted to be found in order to tell the world that she had not been guilty of what she did; of having an abortion. Later she decided there was no use to it. Rebecca and the Leader had both talked to the woman but she had her free agency. This means that if someone asks you to do something you can refuse as each of us has the power to make our own choices. The Leader told the woman that to be found would benefit others in many ways, that it would help many people, but the woman said she didn't want anything else to do with it, and her free agency could not be taken away.

On July 29, 1964, Rebecca said her Leader had a surprise for me but He wouldn't tell her what it was. She said it would help me but she didn't think it was anything connected with finding the body. On October 6, she said my surprise was coming soon.

On October 18, 1964, I got my surprise. At that time I had been married almost twenty-five years. During all of those years my sexual activity was quite limited, as my wife believed that sex was for reproduction only. In an instant this attitude changed, giving us both pleasure and an understanding we had not known before. I asked my wife the reason for this sudden change, and she said, "I don't know; it just came into my mind". On October 19, Rebecca said her Leader had told her that I had received my surprise but He still wouldn't tell her what it was.

The very first time I contacted Rebecca, she told me that not only was I privileged to be able to talk to her but that I must be someone special because the Leader wanted to talk to me. Others have hypnotized Irene but no one, not even my teacher "The Baron" had ever been able to regress her and make contact with Rebecca. Was this a privilege I earned prior to coming into this life? Does it have anything to do with my level of spiritual knowledge and beliefs? Is it connected to the purpose of my present life? After all these years I still don't understand how or why I was privileged to have been given this knowledge and experience which is apparently rare in the process of hypnotism. Thirty-five years of additional experiences in hypnotic regression have never diminished the impact and knowledge it imparted.

It was the result of these regressions that caused me to leave the search for the body in the mountains unfinished. I chose to devote my time to exploring the unknown depths of the mind and I found that I was getting knowledge far more important than finding the body of a missing woman. Subsequent regressions with Irene and several others were compiled and published in my first book.

I held regressions with several other subjects and comparisons were made of the answers from each individual. What one person said about a particular subject was confirmed by another. I continued to build patterns, which I find are consistent with all subjects in hypnotic regression. Years of exploration have only confirmed my original findings. The following is a review of some of that material

During my first regression with Irene I asked Rebecca if she and Irene were the same person. She answered, "I could say yes and I could say no. Yes, I am the same person, but I am further ahead in time. No, I am she, but only after she has learned. And no, because I am not with her exactly. I have gone further; we will unite later".

I took this same question to another person in regression who said, "I am what I am, but I also have a reflection of what I am. In time we become the same." It is my opinion that they were both saying the same thing.

After Rebecca left for another part of her mission I attempted to make contact with her again without success. It was not until December 3, 1964, that I was able to reach her again at which time Rebecca said she had attempted to contact me again through a companion but had not been successful. In discussing her mission she indicated that she had discovered many things about herself. She learned she had a twin sister who was one step below her. She had lived four previous lives and her twin was from one of them. She also went back to the area of the missing woman and looked for her but couldn't find her. Various subjects were discussed but mainly we talked about her mission, and about my talking with the Leader. She said her mission was coming to a close.

Rebecca described her realm as being "beyond": beyond the earth, beyond my understanding, just beyond. She described the realm as being very beautiful, and that the privileged were there to help people who were far away, beyond, to help them to understand and learn. They have a leader who leads them in the things to do and not to do. She tried to explain the different areas in the "Beyond". Apparently each area or level has a low, medium, and high plane.

She said the purpose in her realm is to help others both in her area and on earth. They do not think of their own pleasures as most of us do, but receive their pleasure by helping others. Rebecca said that in her realm they use fewer, more meaningful words in their communication and that in our language we use so many unnecessary words that have no meaning.

The realm between lives is always described as beautiful, like paradise. Everyone there is dressed in a garment that is styled to have a meaning to his level and station. I learned that a short brown sackcloth robe represents a novice. A white robe with a red belt means that entity is about to be born into a new physical life experience. A white robe with a blue sash across the right shoulder to the left hip is a teacher. One trimmed in gold braid means the entity is an advanced teacher, or one of superior knowledge. Everyone has duties, and each one barters his services. The male is looked up to and is considered above the female in intelligence. She said it was proper that women should always look up to men, and that for a woman to overpower a man is wrong, as it will one day bring disaster. Women are becoming more intelligent and are doing men's work which causes men to do women's work and this causes much unhappiness.

During our discussions I asked Rebecca about death. She said that going ahead, or dying, is decided by the Leader and the individual. This will be done when the individual is finished with a phase of his/her learning. When a person no longer has the will to live the Leader contacts them and they talk about it. If He feels that the individual is no longer helping himself/herself he will let this individual go ahead to another level. If necessary, He will also help the person have the will or desire to live. This is done at a level of consciousness far beyond the person's conscious awareness.

When asked to explain birth Rebecca said that this is when the Leader sends a Soul. When the decision is made to enter the physical world a Soul is selected and given records about the people to whom it will be born. After it decides and agrees to be born the soul studies these records and makes another decision as to whether or not it desires to carry on. There are no names, only a code. Being born is like dying and dying is like being born. (The manner in which this statement was made indicated it is simply a process of moving from one experience to another.) Rebecca further stated that the Soul may not want to continue this experience during the period between conception and birth and, in this case, the result would be a miscarriage. When the Soul leaves the physical body there is no more life in the body. This suggests that the Soul, at any level, is selected or chooses to be born into a new physical life for the purpose and benefit of someone else, or for the purpose of experiencing and proving to itself things that will raise it to higher levels of perfection in the process of again becoming one with God (The Leader).

Rebecca was asked about suicide and about war. She replied that suicide is a sin for only God has the right to take a life. Taking a life in a war, or fighting for your country against another country, is another situation. Of course many people in war kill their fellow men when it is not necessary but then they pay for this in their own torment. She said there had been a war in her area, not a war of weapons but a war of words. This war was between Lucifer and Christ. I said that history showed that Christ won that war. She said no. This war was arbitrated by God who decided that Christ would come to our world to save the people.

I asked how she felt about predestination, as to whether or not she believed it. "Yes, things don't just happen, things are planned. Every life that is taken is planned. No matter how it happens, everything is planned. Most things are planned so you can learn. If you leave one place and go to another, it is so you can learn. You have your free agency and ability to learn. You don't have to take that trip. I'm not saying they are planned, say, a hundred years before they happen, but they are planned as you go along. Everything you do, even if you just scratch your head, is all recorded, every bit, even when you are asleep."

I questioned one male adult in regression about predestination and his answer was, "At any given moment infinite possibilities are possible and yet only one becomes actual and, at that stage of becoming actual, one could say it's predestined. Before that nothing is predestined".

"Whom He did predestine, them He also called; and whom He called, them He also glorified" (Romans 9:30).

"Having predestined us, being predestined according to the purpose of Him who worketh all things after the counsel of His will" (Ephesians 1:5).

I asked about religion, wanting to find out the "true" religion. Rebecca said that I would have to find this out myself. She said, "I'll tell you one thing, it's exactly like it was in the beginning. It's never changed".

When Rebecca was questioned about the Bible, she called it "The Book of The Leader" stating, "We don't exactly go by it. We are here, as He is, to help others. We know what we are supposed to know about Him".

We discussed future events and world conditions. She predicted the re-election of President Lyndon Johnson. When he was re-elected I suggested that her prediction wasn't really that amazing because of the thousands of other people who thought the same way. She said, "But they weren't sure and I was".

In many of my hypnotic regressions my subjects spoke of vibrations. One subject said that, on death, the Soul takes on a higher vibration and rises, goes to God, and is formed into another body, a spiritual one of higher vibrations. Another subject, when asked if he knew who he was talking to said, "I have talked to you before. I recognize your vibrations". Another, when asked the same question said, "I know your essence".

When I started one regression the subject said I had interrupted him. He was trying to listen to Christ who was teaching a class. He said, "He comes around and touches everyone of us to pass His vibrations on to us and He becomes very white. He expands Himself and then touches us on the forehead and it feels real good. He is able to generate a lot of energy. He expands his aura, His vibrations. It's like breathing in a way. He expands it more and more and His light becomes brighter. We can identify each other by our vibrations."

The colors spoken of as belonging to the "astral plane" or "astral world" are believed to be vibrations between 20 and 40 trillions per second and can only be seen by those who have developed their psychic abilities. The mental effects of these vibrations can be recognized by the expressions, "It's a dark time," "I feel blue," "I am green with envy," "Looking through rose-colored glasses," etc. The violets, said to be 700 billions per second, denote religion and intuition. Blues, 600 billions per second, denote intellect and reason. Reds, 400 billions per second, denote passion and activity. Greens show union and strength. Yellows show age and weakness. Blacks and grays are inactivity and depression. Whites are purity and zeal.

Dr. Patrick O'Donnell has stated that by seeing through a film of certain chemicals between sheets of glass, the radiations around the body, called the aura, become visible. He says at the moment of death the light begins to spread from the body and rapidly disappears.

Rebecca informed me during a regression with Irene, that arrangements had been made and completed for me to talk with the Leader. I was given a fourteen-day period to select a time and date. The date selected was February 20, 1965. I was told the visit would not be a social one; I was to prepare a list of questions, which would be answered for me. I was permitted to ask any question on any subject. The result of this regression is covered in the next chapter.

Let me ask you, the reader, to contemplate what questions you would ask if you were offered an invitation to talk to God? Can you picture yourself discussing such an appointment openly with your friends? What reaction do you think you would receive from such an announcement?

Chapter Eight
THE LEADER

(A Conversation With God)

After the evolved spirit Rebecca, told me that she would bring God to answer my questions I wanted to be prepared for this experience so I sought the advice and opinions of others as to what it meant and what they thought about the responses I was getting in hypnotic regressions. I talked with friends, doctors, ministers and the man on the street. I asked them what they would say if they were able to talk directly to God. What kind of questions would they ask of Him? The reactions I got from these people were quite discouraging. Most would look at me with pity or react as if I were some kind of nut or thought I was joking with them. When the time came for the actual experience I was still very much unprepared. It was February 20, 1965. Irene's mother was always present during these regressions and assisted in preparing the questions we asked. Irene was placed in hypnosis and Rebecca was contacted in the usual manner.

Me:	"Rebecca?"
Rebecca:	"Yes."
Me:	"Is everything ready?"
Rebecca:	"Yes."
Me:	"Boy!"
Rebecca:	"You don't believe it, huh?"
Me:	"It's hard to believe. I'm nervous."
Rebecca:	"I'll have to send for Him, He's not right here."
Me:	"I understand. I wonder if you would like to visit some before you do this"?
Rebecca:	"Yes, while I'm sending for Him, we can visit. Can you wait just a minute?" Pause... "Are you there?"
Me:	"Have you talked with the Leader since you last talked to me?"
Rebecca:	"Yes."

Me:	"Did He have anything to say about this visit?"
Rebecca:	"No, except He was looking forward to it."
Me:	"I have prepared some questions as you told me to do. I think you will find we have discussed some of them before. I already have your opinion on them. Some of them you told me that I should talk to Him about."
Rebecca:	"Yes, I remember."
Me:	"We talked about changing sex and colors in different life experiences. I have found this to happen in other regressions."
Rebecca:	"You found what?"
Me:	"Well, for instance, during a regression with one woman she described a life in 1425, as a woman, then as we moved ahead in time to the year 1705 she described herself as a man. I have a question about this. Some of these past experiences being described may not be the truth, or may not be their own."
Rebecca:	"Well, anything you have doubts about you should ask Him to straighten things out."
Me:	"How long do you think it will take for Him to get here?"
Rebecca:	"He should be here any time now. He's not far."
Me:	"Tell me how you sent for Him."
Rebecca:	"By a messenger."
Me:	"Are there messengers with you all the time?"
Rebecca:	"No, they fly around all over the place."
Me:	"They what?"
Rebecca:	"Fly—they are birds."
Me:	"Oh! That's how you do it. Are they doves or pigeons?"
Rebecca:	"They are white. They are messengers."
Me:	"How do you call them? Do you have to catch one, or signal to them?"
Rebecca:	"No, they just come up to you. They are all over the place. I usually carry one around on my shoulder."
Me:	"What is called, or considered, an Angel?"
Rebecca:	"Angel?"

Me:	"Yes, on earth we refer to God's helpers as Angels."
Rebecca:	"We are God's helpers, but we don't call ourselves that. We just call ourselves helpers."
Me:	"Am I to understand that in addition to Jesus Christ and God there are other people in your Realm called Masters? Others who have made similar contribution in our area such as Buddha And Mohammed. Do you know these persons?"
Rebecca:	"No, I don't understand your Masters. We have Masters, I guess you could call them that. See the way it is, we have the Leader and the Teacher and then we have those who go to your area quite frequently to give a person a message or something like that. I mean, we usually don't,
	we the helpers, just help from here. You know what I mean."
Me:	"Am I to understand that the person I am to talk with is the Leader and not Christ?"
Rebecca:	"Yes, the Leader. The Teacher is off on a mission and I was hoping that both of them could be here. You could see the difference and everything, but He is working and He's very seldom available."
Me:	"This study and mission you are going on, are you still working on it?"
Rebecca:	"Oh yes. I'll be working on it every chance I get."
Me:	"I've been thinking. You told me that when you go on this mission you will be born into another life experience, yet you would still be with Irene. I don't understand how this is possible."
Rebecca:	"Well, I will be born into a life experience with a body, but I also have a Soul, you know."
Me:	"Yes."
Rebecca:	"And this Soul will be with me and will also be watching over her."
Me:	"What about the body you are born to? Where will that soul come in? Won't that body have a Soul also?"
Rebecca:	"That's what I said."
Me:	"I don't understand."
Rebecca:	"I said I will have a body and I will have a Soul. That Soul

75

will be with the body and also be watching over Irene, sort of like two Souls. There's part of that Soul that will be with me but still be watching over her."

Me: "Do you have any way of knowing if you will be born as a member of Irene's family, or if you will have any association with her in this new experience?"

Rebecca: "It would be very unlikely that I will be associated at all with her."

Me: "This is what I can't understand, how being apart from her so much you can still watch over her and somebody else also."

Rebecca: "It's not hard. There was a case here where a person took a life experience and when he came back he told some of us that he had watched over twenty different people. So it's not impossible. This is just a little step."

Me: "Confusion, confusion."

Rebecca: "I don't think you would really understand, even if I took a long time to explain it. Excuse me." Pause...."The Leader is here now. The way we will work this is you will tell me what you want to know, and it will appear to you that I will be pausing, but I will be telling Him in my language, so it will be faster, and then He will tell me and I will tell you. Is that all right?"

Me: "Yes, I understand. That will be fine. (How else would we do it?) Before I get into my questions I want to express my thanks and appreciation for the good life He has given me. Also I am very much aware of the surprise that was given me."

Rebecca: "Oh yeah! Just a second." Pause...."He said that He is very well pleased with you, and that He knows that you are very humble. He said that you have received your surprise, so I guess you know."

Note: During this regression Rebecca listened to my questions. Irene's lips moved but no sound came from her and after a pause, Rebecca would give me an answer. The expression on Irene's face was just as if she were talking to someone. After waiting for His response she talked to me.

Me: "The first question I have is about the truth of past life

	experiences as described by others in regression. Are they authentic?"
Rebecca:	"If they are the truth?" Pause...."Usually what you hear from the mouths of other people whom you have regressed is usually the truth. He unveils certain things to you so you will learn. This is a learning process. Sometimes He hast hem not remember, or He doesn't reveal to
	them as much as they would like to know. You have to determine which is which. He leaves that up to you."
Me:	"I understand then that I should continue to do
	this and take advantage of the opportunities to develop my knowledge in this?"
Rebecca:	Pause.... "Yes."
Me:	"How can I develop more ability and understanding about this in order to inform others of this knowledge so they can learn as I have?"
Rebecca:	"So you can teach, in other words?"
Me:	"Yes."
Rebecca:	Pause and laughter...."He says by learning more, to study, and have patience and faith. Does that tell you anything?"
Me:	"I understand. You indicated that you would be leaving in a few months. I feel badly about this. I wonder if there will be a possibility for me to make contact with someone who can help me the same as you have?"
Rebecca:	"Through a different person?"
Me:	"I assume it would have to be with another person since you are leaving. I wonder if there is a way I can communicate with somebody in your area as privileged as you?"
Rebecca:	Pause..."No."
Me:	"Is there a reason for this?"
Rebecca:	"He said that one such experience as this is enough."
Me:	(Personally I don't think one such experience is ever enough.)
Rebecca:	"Ask if there is something I can do while I still have this opportunity, while I still have this advantage. Is there something I can attempt or have?"

Me: Pause…"He says to ask anything you want on any subject, this way you will learn."

Rebecca: "Ask Him if He has talked directly to others in my area."

Me: Pause… "Yes."

Rebecca: "When we pray, does it make any difference what pattern we follow? Is there a prayer of thanks, or a request for help acknowledged, and must a prayer be spoken aloud?"

Me: Pause…"He said He can hear a prayer even if it is just a thought. Like a person is drowning and that person is thinking, Help. He can hear this.Do you understand?"

Rebecca: "Yes, I understand."

Me: "He can hear any prayer spoken aloud, or a thought from a person not even knowing it, but thinking he needs help without knowing it. He can hear this."

Rebecca: "Getting back to regression and the change in sex in different life experiences. If such a thing happens, what would be the reason for this?"

Me: "Then they can regress into the lives of their ancestors?"

Rebecca: Pause…"Yes."

For three years I fought with this response. Regressions have always shown there could have been a change of sex and race in past lives. It was not until I read <u>A Course in Miracles</u> that I found an explanation. We were created as free spirits in the likeness of God. As free spirits, we can choose to experience a physical life, and we can create ourselves in any gender, in any type experience we want. When we return to the spiritual realm we become the original gender in which we were created.

Me: "I still can't understand why I have the honor or privilege to talk to Him."

Rebecca: Pause…"He said that you are honored in this way but that He has talked to other people in your area so you are not the only person. He has never talked through so many people to get to you like this. He said that the reason is for you to learn and Him to…I don't know what you call

it, <u>experiment</u> I guess you would say."

Me: "Then I am to believe that it is His desire or opinion that I should continue to improve myself in this line of work?"

Rebecca: Pause…"Yes."

Me: "Now that this has happened, and even with all the information I have been given, few people are going to believe this. Very few people are going to be convinced that such a thing has taken place. Is there anything I can have or do that will prove that this has really happened?"

Rebecca: Pause…"He said that to prove this would be hard. The only thing you can tell a person who does not believe is to tell him, hasn't the Leader and Teacher talked to others? Hasn't it been known that they have talked to people such as you before? Give examples. You must know some. He will help as much as He can in having the person believe you. You will just have to take the chance and try to prove to them as much as you can. This is another learning process."

Me: "Ask Him if there are any instructions or thoughts He would like to give me before He leaves."

Rebecca: Pause…"He said to learn so that you will be able to come to my house. Learn, learn, learn, and remember that no man is an island." Pause…"Are you still there?"

Me: "I'm at a loss for words to say. I appreciate His time, His help, and would hope I could have opportunities to do this again in the future."

Rebecca: "You mean talk to Him again?"

Me: "Yes. To let Him know I'm trying, that I want to do the right things."

Rebecca: "Do you want me to ask Him if you can talk to Him again?"

Me: "Well, yes."

Rebecca: Pause…"He said that in talking to Him again, He didn't know if this would be possible because He's very busy. But, He will try to get the Teacher to come and talk to you at least once before I go on my mission, if he can arrange it, so that you will have two different…you know. He says it has been a great pleasure for Him to talk with you even if it hasn't been direct and that He must go now and, if you have anything to leave with Him, do it at this time."

Me: "I have one more question. I wonder if there is anything He could tell me that I'm doing wrong, anything that I can

	improve myself in?"
Rebecca:	"Yes, I understand." Pause…"Hummmmmm…He said that He cannot tell you what you are doing wrong. That you have to find this out for yourself, that He doesn't think you have anything especially that you are doing wrong, but for you to be looking at yourself continually and concentrate on what you are doing and this way you can see your own mistakes and learn by them."
Me:	"Thank Him again if He's leaving now."
Rebecca:	"And He said—Just a minute." Pause…"And He said He understands how you feel about being able to talk to Him, that you need not use words to express, that He can understand. Now what do you want me to tell Him?"
Me:	"That's all. I just wanted to say thanks again."
Rebecca:	Pause…"He says He has been honored by this visit and good-bye." Pause…."I am back."
Me:	"Okay, now you can talk with me. What do you think?"
Rebecca:	"What do I think about the meeting?"
Me:	"Yes."
Rebecca:	"I think it was successful. I know He has enjoyed it Himself. He is going to see about you talking to the Teacher if you want to."
Me:	"Of course."
Rebecca:	"It might be some time you know. Right now He's gone and it might be that He might not even be able to. So don't worry if He doesn't. I think it has been a good meeting. He hasn't told you not to ask Him certain questions for which He wouldn't give you the answers. I know sometimes when I ask Him, He just says, 'I can't answer that for you; you have to find the answer for yourself.' I figured He would be telling you that most of the time." Laughter… I think the reason He did this was because He wanted you to learn from the experience, and I think you have. He was sort of experimenting with this and I think He got whatever He wanted out of the experience because He was very well pleased."
Me:	"In your opinion, did I ask the proper questions or should I have…"

Rebecca: "Yes, you asked anything you wanted. There were no set questions that you had to ask Him."

Me: "Well, you know this was a very difficult thing to do."

Rebecca: "Yes I know."

Me: "I mean it was difficult to think of something."

Rebecca: "I could feel you were…how do you put it? He's not really very talkative either. He's direct, everything is direct. He doesn't do like I do. I tell Him something and He just… it comes out just as fast as lightning. You know, He has the answer ready and waiting."

Me: "I have often wondered, and I have asked this of others. If you were to ask a question of God, and He would be right there to give you an answer, what would you ask? Very few people know what they would do under these circumstances."

Rebecca: "It's not easy. I can imagine how difficult it is for you when it is difficult for me sometimes, because He is so far above me in intelligence. Sometimes I think He's going to think I'm stupid if I ask a certain question, but He's very understanding and direct."

Me: "I don't know when I will have the opportunity to talk with you again. Tell me if you will continue to be available."

Rebecca: "Yes. Until a couple of days before my mission, then I will be so busy that I won't want to talk about it."

Me: "This mission, did you say it will occur in May or June?"

Rebecca: "June. I have found out the day that I will be leaving. If I give it to you then you won't try to get me anymore after that. It will be the 28th of June. I probably won't be able to talk to anyone at all. I imagine you can understand this? I would like it very much though if you could talk to me the 18th, or 19th. When I say contact me one more time before I go, then I will give you the date. I hate to cut this short but I have to go and pick flowers. I have to pick flowers and take them to the Leader. It's my time, my turn, so I will go now. Is there anything else you want to ask me before I go?"

I don't mind saying that this regression left me emotionally shaken. It would be most difficult to explain my feelings resulting from this experience.

While doing these regressions with the girl Irene I had feelings of doubt and feelings of belief. I turned to others in hypnosis and regression to verify or disprove the information I was getting. My hypnosis instructor, Baron Von Brenner, told me that in his thirty-three years of being a master hypnotist; he had never experienced some of the things I was doing with hypnosis. There had to be an explanation behind this phenomenon so I sought the opinion of others in the fields of psychology and parapsychology. Mr. Hugh Lynn Cayce, son of Edgar Cayce, gave me an hour of his time and after he had listened to my experiences in hypnotic regression put his hands in the air and said, "The mind does many strange and wonderful things". The he left me to my own evaluation of this event. I could not find anyone else to show me that such an experience had happened before or why it had happened to me. I know this experience made a definite change in my life. As the Leader suggested, I began to look at myself, concentrating on what I do and why. I turned to religious studies of all kinds and began to understand a real purpose for life and what I must do to prepare myself for my life with God.

Chapter Nine
LEGAL ASPECTS OF HYPNOTISM

On March 13, 1965 I had a regression with Irene with several people present. One was a woman who had outstanding abilities as a psychic medium.

During my many years of investigation and research in the field of hypnotism I have met many who profess to be adapt in some manner of psychic ability. I have met only a few whom I believe were authentic in their psychic expressions.

Our psychic guest, my brother, and I were the only ones that Irene was able to hear and talk with during these regressions. Irene placed in the hypnotic condition and contact was made with Rebecca.

Me.	Rebecca! How have you been?
Rebecca.	Fine. How have you been?
Me.	I have been having quite a time since our last meeting. Nobody wants to believe me when I tell them what happened at our last regression, about talking to the Leader.
Rebecca.	Well. What have you done to have them believe you?
Me.	I'm working on it. Tell me, do you know of other planets that have life such as we have?
Rebecca.	Yes. All of them have a form of life.
Me.	Would you know if the life is similar to ours in intelligence?
Rebecca.	Well, some of them closer to the Sun, as close as we are here and you are there wouldn't be as high an intelligence as the Earth, but they have life that carries on.
Me.	It has been interpreted by science writers that life on other planets may be in the form of vegetation or animal types rather than human form as we have.
Rebecca.	On some of them, Yes.
Me.	Do you mean this actually exists?

Rebecca.	Yes. Don't you believe me?
Me.	No. I wouldn't say that.
Rebecca.	Of course I don't come in contact with other worlds too much, but I know this from the Leader and Teacher. My contacts are mostly to your world.
Me.	The last time we visited you indicated that I might have the opportunity to talk with the Teacher.
Rebecca.	Yes. I was talking to the Leader not too long ago, a couple of days ago, and He said the Teacher is gone out doing something right now, and if you do get to talk to him it would have to be later.
Me.	The girl's (Irene) mother would like to contact you. She has tried twice without success. Is there a reason she can't reach you?
Rebecca.	I don't know, maybe she has to learn more. There is something not completed. Not everyone can reach me.
Me.	Just because someone knows hypnosis and how to use it does not mean they can contact you?
Rebecca.	No. I have had no one but you do it.
Me.	What about my brother? (My brother Richard was present at a regression with Irene) The unusual results are recorded on page fifty-three of my book, "The Inner Mind".
Rebecca.	There was something wrong there. It was very faint. Something wasn't right.
Me.	This makes me feel honored.
Rebecca.	You are just privileged I guess.
Me.	Many people think those who work with hypnotism are weird.
Rebecca.	They don't understand. What they don't understand throw aside. I predict your teachings will become more and more essential. It will be used all over. This is not magic. People fear what they don't know. It will spread and in the future be used very much. My opinion is that you should set up an organization and teach. You should teach this and make it a life's work.
Me.	How do you feel about predestination? Do you believe

	this?
Rebecca.	Yes. Things just don't happen. Things are planned. Every life that is taken, this is planned. No matter how it happens, everything is planned.
Me.	Does this include personal things, like affection and love for another?
Rebecca.	Yes. Most things are planned so you can learn. If you leave a place and go to another it is so you can learn.
Me.	If it's all planned where is our free agency, or the ability to reason?
Rebecca.	You decide. You don't have to take that trip. I'm not saying they are planned; say a hundred years before they happen. They are planned as we go.
Me.	In living a life, each life you gain a certain amount of knowledge. Are all of this recorded and the record kept somewhere?
Rebecca.	Everything you do, even if you just scratch your head, it's all recorded, every bit, even if you're asleep. To me it works like a telephone, you just have this ability. Some people have this ability all the time, others don't.
Me.	Okay. While we are talking there are other people here listing.
Rebecca.	Yes I know. I feel that one person who is with you is very close to me. I don't know...I feel a bright light, a warm light in the presence that I have never felt before. I feel that a person is there that is close to me and my surroundings here.

(Rebecca was referring to the woman with the psychic abilities.)

Me.	You're right. This person has demonstrated he psychic abilities to me.
Rebecca.	Uh huh, yes. Well she is very gifted and very privileged or she wouldn't be able to do this.
Me.	Would it be possible for her to talk to you? Could she ask you a question?
Rebecca.	You mean not going through you. I don't know if I could or not. She can try.

Me.	Do I tell the truth when I say that I see Christ?
Rebecca.	Well I imagine she does tell the truth. I'm not doubting her word. There are a lot of people who see Him. There are a lot of people who say, "Who does that person thing they are".
Me.	You mean like me? Who do I think I am to be able to talk to your Leader? Why should this happen to me?
Rebecca.	Well. In your book, what do you call it? The Bible. He talked to people just like I talk to you, but He sees them, they see each other so why shouldn't He be able to do it now? What would change it? There are more years but it doesn't change the person. Say you are twenty and twenty years from now you're going to be the same person. You might have a different outlook but you're still the same person as a whole.
Me.	Nothing is making them so aware today as it did at that time. That may be why they feel what happened is not possible,
Rebecca.	Also, they put Him so far ahead of them, put Him on a pedestal so far above them that they can't comprehend Him lowering to the same level, as they are to talk.
Me.	Am I to understand that the souls, or people in your area, have a good contact with the people in my area most of the time, even though we are not aware of this?
Rebecca.	Oh yes. They are there all the time. You can't see them but they are around. Let me give you an example. I have a friend here, and he said that one day he was with his mother, or sister, and this person was sort of upset and started to walk out into the street and a car came by and she looked up just in time to move. What happened was that he told her mind, or whatever you want to call it, to look up, but she didn't know this. She thought she did it on her own, but this way he helped her, so they're always around.
Me.	Do some people have the ability to see them?
Rebecca.	Oh yes.
Me.	Many people and religions have recognized Christ as an individual, but look upon God as nothing more than total

energy, or a higher vibration.

Rebecca. Yes. They can't comprehend it because, see the Teacher came to Earth and there are records of this. People are going to believe this more. The Leader didn't do like the Teacher so it is going to be harder for them to understand.

Me. The lady you feel close to you, do you have any thoughts about her?

Rebecca. No really, I just feel her presence and I can hear her.

Me. I'm wondering how she is so free to talk to me about the future and you don't want to do that for me.

Rebecca. Well, everybody's different. She might not be so close to the Leader and Teacher as I am. She might not know what they want you to know and what they don't want you to know, and I do. If she gets her information she might tell you everything. I know there are lots of things she doesn't tell you.

Me. There was a piece in this morning paper about hypnosis and the laws.

Rebecca. Yes. I don't know them but I know about them,

Me. There is an assemblyman who has introduced a bill in our state that would prohibit people like me from using hypnotism. It would prohibit hypnotism by other than medical personnel.

Rebecca. Oh hog wash. I would fight it. I would call up the newspaper and give them an article that would make his ears ring. You're a citizen aren't you? In your paper don't they have a place where people can give opinions?

Me. Yes.

Rebecca. Well! Write them a letter and tell them. In a way think of it. There are a lot of people that use this practice that aren't doctors and they are just as good in it, or probable better you can understand this because people are scared to have anything to do with it unless it's a doctor because doctors are professionals. I would write them a letter and tell them what I than any doctor. I would tell them, and this could be helping you also. If you write in and told them then people would read it. I wouldn't stop at anything. You know they say if you don't like something

	in your government change it. You're the people.
Me.	How would a person prepare himself or herself to go to your area?
Rebecca.	Learn as much as you can. You don't have to be.... I know a lot of people that were doctors and lawyers and teachers that aren't here. You don't have to be a certain profession to be here.It's how much you learn in your life that counts. I know people who have never had an occupation higher than a laborer that have learned.
Me.	I have a question for your Teacher. Recently I saw a movie of the life of Christ. Some of the material seems to indicate that when he was crucified he was nailed to the cross with the nails through the palms of His hands.
Rebecca.	Yes. His feet, and His sides.
Me.	There are some indications that the nails were not through the palms but through his wrists. Would you know?
Rebecca.	I don't think so. I will ask Him. I'm pretty sure that it was His palms, feet, and sides.
Me.	Would you know why there is very little record or information available about the time Christ was a child and before He appeared to teach his disciples?
Rebecca.	Because this time was not important. This was His growing period. He had nothing to do at this time but learn.
Me.	I better let you go, so goodbye.
Rebecca.	Yes, I think I had better go. I have some flowers to pick, and I want to talk to the Leader. It's been good talking to you and your associates.

Because of my interest in hypnosis and the actions that are being taken, and the attempts to control its uses, I have asked related questions of all my subjects in regression. I have found they are all of the opinion that hypnosis is a science of its own, and a profession should not control it where its uses would be restricted. Also, certain people seem to be gifted with the knowledge and ability of helping others to understand things about themselves and their purpose in life.

Several laws have been drafted and submitted to the law making bodies of several states throughout the nation by the American Medical Association in an attempt to control the use of hypnotism. These bills tend to exclude from the practice those who have made hypnotism their profession many years before the A.M.A. recognized that hypnotism was something more than a parlor game. I know many members of the Medical Association who have taken as few as six hours of instruction in hypnotism and then offered their services as professionals in the subject. These same people are among the first to condemn the lay hypnotist while attempting to gain control of its uses.

I agree there should be laws, controls and qualification standards for the use of hypnotism but not to restrict its use by any one group or profession. These laws and qualifications should be for the purpose of placing hypnotism on a professional level so schools and businesses can be opened to offer the services of hypnotism without the practitioner being harassed by those who would like to control all human activity.

Reviewing the above statements brings to mind an old, old comment made by Thomas Jay Hudson LL.D in his book, "The Law of Psychic Phenomena" Copyrighted in 1893. I quote from pages 141,142,and 143.

"It is thought that enough has been said to show that the dangers attending the practice of hypnotism have been greatly exaggerated, and that the sources of danger, which people are so persistently warned against, have no existence in fact. The premises laid down will not be gainsaid by any who understand the law of suggestion. The conclusions are inevitable. The law of autosuggestion has been recognized by continental writers, as has been shown by extracts from their books; but they have failed to carry it to its legitimate conclusion when treating the subject of the legal aspects of hypnotism. It is perhaps not strange that they should fail in this respect, in view of the vital interest, which physicians have in hypnotism as a therapeutic agent. But they should remember that the subject is also of vital interest to students of psychology, and that it is only a study of its psychological aspects that hypnotism can be intelligently applied to the cure of disease. That the phenomena displayed through its agency possess a significance, which transcends that which attaches to it as a substitute for pills, is a proposition, which will not be disputed, even by those who seek to monopolize its forces. It is hoped, therefore, that the psychological student will be graciously permitted to pursue his studies at least until it is shown that physicians enjoy such monopoly of the cardinal virtues that it is unsafe to entrust the forces of nature in the hands of others".

"In the meantime the world at large will continue to believe that the laws of hypnotism are no exception of the rule that the forces of nature, when once understood, are designed for the highest good of mankind; and they will continue to demand that those forces shall not be monopolized by any man, or set of men, body, politic or corporation".

"From what has been said, the supreme folly of legislation to prohibit experiments in hypnotism is manifest. No one will deny that when a hypnotist permits himself to exercise his art in private he is in possession of opportunities which, under other conditions, might give him undue advantages over a subject of the opposite sex, but, from the very nature of things, that advantage is infinitely less than that enjoyed by physicians in their habitual intercourse with their patients. Until it is shown that physicians never take advantage of their confidential relations with their patients; until it is shown that physicians are exempt from human passions and frailties; or at least, until it is shown that physicians are more platonic in their emotions than the ordinary run of human beings, the world will continue to regard their demand that the study of experimental psychology, as an exhibition of monumental impudence".

"It cannot be forgotten that it was the medical profession that drove Mesmer into dishonored exile and a premature grave for the sole reason that he healed the sick without the use of pills. The faculty ridiculed, prescribed, and ostracized every medical man who dared to conduct an honest investigation of mesmeric phenomena. And now that scientists of Europe are compelled to admit the therapeutic value of the science, they are instant in demand that no one but physicians shall be permitted to make experiments. It is perhaps natural and right that the treatment of disease by means of drugs should be restricted to those who are educated in the proper use of drugs; but the employment of psychic powers and remedies rests upon an entirely different footing. Their demand that hypnotism be reserved for their exclusive use rests not upon knowledge of its laws, but is founded upon their willful ignorance of the fundamental principles which underlie the science".

It would seem that professional groups and the established attitudes within these groups seldom change, and that man's attitudes and his manner of living changes only when he moves from one to another profession, or until he investigates and studies the knowledge outside of his own profession. The attitudes of the medical profession concerning hypnotism today are not much different from what they were in the year 1893, even though over one hundred years of experience has proven the lack of validity of their arguments.

The material in this book should add to the proof that there does exist a link, or association, between the physical life of man and the spiritual realm from whence he came. Hypnotism is a means of making man aware of this association, and of bringing out the powers, which heal the physical, mental, and spiritual ills of them who need and desire this help. It is a means of fulfilling the demands of God that we recognize this source of power within us. A close review of the information given by those in the attitude of hypnotic regression will prove there is an inner knowledge, which transcends the comprehension of the individual's conscious awareness.

A few years ago Alan W. Scheflin and Jerrold Lee Shapero co-authored a book called, "Trance On Trial" which was published by the Guilford Press. They have covered the laws and attitudes concerning hypnotism of each of the United States that have found it necessary to make a commitment about this expression. At the present time Indiana is the only state to enact a law licensing the use of hypnosis. Again this law seems to favor those who get their training from a certain school that was influential in getting the law passed.

California has a certification system. Schools have to meet certain qualifications for the training of those interested in hypnosis as a profession, or as a supplement to other expressions in the healing arts. Originally Certification was given for just a few hours of training. Today these schools require as much as three hundred hours of training at a cost between $1500.00 and $2500.00 for a certification. This certification restricts the use of hypnotism to non-medical conditions unless; the practitioner is licensed in the medical profession.

My approach in the use of hypnotist is to allow the individual to Heal him or her self. Working with the hypothesis that everything experienced has been recorded and retained, I found that the mind not only contains the knowledge of life, and the purpose for its existence and conduct, it also contains the answers for its own improvement of emotional, physical, and spiritual conditions. I have shown that any of these conditions, as to the origin, cause and solution, can be fully evaluated in a one-hour hypnotic session, and without the client speaking a word.

Chapter Ten
THE TEACHER

(A Conversation with Jesus)

During one of my regressions with Irene Rebecca told me the Teacher would be available for a visit with me during a nine-day period. I was to select the time and date for this visit and the Teacher would talk with me about anything I wanted to ask. However, I was still not prepared when the time came.

Even after all these years of doing hypnotic regressions and looking into the many different religions, I was still not fully prepared to ask questions under the same circumstances as with talking to God. I know now what one of my subjects in regression meant when he said, "Words kill the Spirit." There is no way to explain the feelings I experienced during the hypnotic sessions of my visits with the Leader and later with the Teacher.

The following regression occurred in May of 1965. Irene was placed in hypnosis and Rebecca was contacted in the usual manner.

Me:	"Rebecca?"
Rebecca:	"Yes."
Me:	"This is the day I am to talk to the Teacher?"
Rebecca:	"Yes."
Me:	"Are we going to work it the same way as we did when I talked to the Leader?"
Rebecca:	"Yes."
Me:	"Do you want to send for Him now?"
Rebecca:	"If you would like."
Me:	"I thought we could visit again like we did before, while we are waiting."
Rebecca:	"All right."
Me:	"I'm excited again. Tell me about talking to Him. Is there anything in particular I should ask Him?"
Rebecca:	"Ask Him anything. It will be similar to the talk you had

	with the Leader except that He might go into more detail. You know He's a teacher and a teacher usually goes into more detail."
Me:	"I have prepared more of a selection of questions. Maybe we can do it easier this time."
Rebecca:	"That's good. Just a minute", Pause…"I'm back."
Me:	"Did you send for Him the same way as you did the Leader? With a bird?"
Rebecca:	"Yes."
Me:	"I had a chance to discuss this experience with a female doctor of psychology. Her first impression was that what I receive in these regressions is only the subject's imagination. After hearing some of my tapes, she said, 'I don't want you to think I believe any of this, but it's something to think about. She said some of her colleagues had discussed such a possibility with her so, who knows, maybe I can cause more interest in this area."
Rebecca:	"Yes. Very good."
	"I also met an eighty-year-old man who has been studying and lecturing on similar phenomena for a long time. He has offered me an introduction to a couple of college professors who teach at a nearby university."
Rebecca:	"I told you, didn't I?"
Me:	"I listen to you even if it is nothing but your imagination."
Rebecca:	"Boy! I've really got an imagination."
Me:	"Why don't you describe where you are right now?"
Rebecca:	"I'm in the garden. I have described it to you before, haven't I?"
Me:	"Yes, by a fence."
Rebecca:	"No. I'm not in that part of the garden. Right now I'm under a big tree. It's one of my favorite spots, looking over the garden, sort of like on a hill."
Me:	"How are you dressed? What kind of clothing do you wear?"
Rebecca:	"Cloth. Long, white cloth."
Me:	"Do most people in your area wear this type dress?"

Rebecca:	"Yes."
Me:	"How are they made? Do you have a place to manufacture them?"
Rebecca:	"Yes, but I wouldn't say manufacture. We have seamstresses who make them for us."
Me:	"I see. Do you have houses and streets? Do you have transportation, such as cars?"
Rebecca:	"Yes, but no cars."
Me:	"Can you describe one of your houses?"
Rebecca:	"Mine I will. I live with three other females. We live in a two-story house with four bedrooms. We have a place to eat. We have a study, one for each. We have a big garden in back. What else do you want to know?"
Me:	"That's fine. What about supplies, such as food?"
Rebecca:	"From people who grow them, yes."
Me:	"It's very similar to how it is in my area."
Rebecca:	"Yes, but it's more united. In your place you give a person something for something, you sort of trade, and this way everyone works together. We divide; I mean we get what we need. We don't, but it's like you do because we don't have anything such as money."
Me:	"In other words you have services, you offer your help if they need it and they offer theirs if you need it?"
Rebecca:	"Yes. You have some of that in some parts of your world, but its not very concrete."
Me:	"You have described your place as being 'beyond.' Would you say you are on another planet, another world, another plane or dimension?"
Rebecca:	"It's not a separate planet. It's sort of a connection with your world. It's like... the only way I can describe it is that it's above your reasoning. I mean it's above you. I really can't make you understand."
Me:	"Well, when people pray and think about being above they think of the heavens, that you would be in the heavens."
Rebecca:	"Yes. Really to them we are in the heavens because we are above them. I mean we are not just in the sky as people think; we are way, way beyond, further than they

can see, but we are above them."

Me: "At what point does the Soul leave the body? When the Soul actually leaves the body is this the cause of death?"

Rebecca: "Well, yes. I guess you could say that because when you have death the Soul leaves. The Soul usually leaves a few seconds before death."

Me: "Where you are, is there division of time between life experiences, like day and night? Light, darkness, and seasons? Do you know time as we know it?"

Rebecca: "Well, yes. The reason for this is that we have our own time, but we have adopted your time because we are always in contact with your people. This way it is easier for everyone."

Me: "Is there any difference in the temperature, hot or cold?"

Rebecca: "It is usually warm all year here."

Me: "Do you experience any pain or illness?"

Rebecca: "Illness yes, but much pain, no."

Me: "Do you have physicians or people to help you over this illness?"

Rebecca: "The Leader and the Teacher and friends."

Me: "In other words it's done more (with)…"

Rebecca: "Feeling."

Me: "More by feeling than it is by medication?"

Rebecca: "No medication."

Me: "How do you occupy your time other than helping people like me?"

Rebecca: "Study. We have our pleasures too. We just don't sit around and study and work. We have different things."

Me: "Men friends?"

Rebecca: "Well, sometimes."

Me: "Do you know how long you have been there in your area?"

Rebecca: "This last time? For about twenty years in your time."

Me: "Are you taught that as you believe it is done unto you? And as a man thinks in his heart so he is?"

Rebecca:	"Yes, that's correct."
Me:	"Do you have to answer for any wrong doing that you might have done in any previous life experience?"
Rebecca:	"No. Not here. You answer for it there."
Me:	"Do you have any idea how long it will be before your Teacher gets here?"
Rebecca:	"He should be here any time now. I don't know where He was. You are getting impatient again."
Me:	"I just wanted to know how much time I have to ask you more questions."
Rebecca:	"Keep asking."
Me:	"This language you use to communicate between yourselves, is it like mine but in fewer words?"
Rebecca:	"Yes."
Me:	"Do you know what the Ten Commandments are?"
Rebecca:	"A set of rules set down by the Leader in the beginning."
Me:	"How were these words given to us?"
Rebecca:	"Through prophets."
Me:	"What about divorce? I'm not sure of the wording in the Bible, but it indicates that Christ was against divorce."
Rebecca:	"There was no divorce in the beginning. I mean you took unto you a wife and you had her until you died or she died."
Me:	"Can you tell me why there is divorce now and not in the beginning, and if it is accepted now?"
Rebecca:	"No, it's not accepted. The reason for this is that people don't know what they want. There are more and more people than there were in the beginning. They are not as God-fearing as they were" Pause..."The Teacher is here."
Me:	"I don't know how to begin our conversation."
Rebecca:	"Just a second...pause...He said that He won't be able to stay long, so if you will get underway then we can get started."
Me:	"Ask Him, when a person takes an interest in the knowledge he may gain spiritually or otherwise, is it because this particular Soul is meant to gain this

knowledge, or he has developed or advanced himself enough to be worthy of obtaining it?"

Rebecca: Pause..."The latter part."

Me: "The miracles that He performed, as we understand them, how was it possible that He could walk on water?"

Rebecca: "I know what you mean." Pause..."He had the power from His Father."

Me: "Would this also pertain to the feeding of the multitudes from the five loaves of bread and two fishes?"

Rebecca: Pause..."Yes."

Me: "Can your Teacher tell me if there is any particular significance as to why I am honored in such a way as to be asking these question of Him?"

Rebecca: "Why you are honored to be able to talk to Him?"

Me: "Yes."

Rebecca: "I don't know the words to say it." Pause...This is another way of helping people in your area."

Me: "Is there anything I can have to help me show or teach that such an experience happened, or is this impossible?"

Rebecca: Pause..."Just be sincere. Make people that you come in contact with, make them feel that you are sincere."

Me: "I understand, but it's very hard for some people to believe that such a thing is possible."

Rebecca: "Oh, you are not going to have everybody understand. I think you have done well so far, don't you?"

Me: "I feel that I have, but I would like..."

Rebecca: "Proof."

Me: "Well, not necessarily proof, but something out of the ordinary, something to improve my ability in helping others. I have worked with many people who have had an illness or deformities. I would like to know if what I have given them has helped them."

Rebecca: "Just a second." Pause..."He says that the more you go (forward), the more power will be released to you in doing this. You will just have to wait and become further advanced. Keep going and more power will be released to

	you. This way you will be able to do what you want to do better and this will be proof enough."
Me:	"Ask Him if we should have fear of passing from one phase of life to another."
Rebecca:	Pause…"No…I knew that."
Me:	"A few weeks ago I talked to a person in regression named Robert. At the time of contact Robert said that he was in a class talking to Christ. Would He know it was I who made contact at that time?"
Rebecca:	"Just a second." Pause… "He said He knows of no contact in His presence."
Me:	"Robert told me that when Christ was born He was given a garment that grew with Him like a living thing, and that He only had this one garment in His entire time on earth. He said that it has been put away in a safe place and in the future will be discovered, which will give us another lesson that Christ was our savior. Ask Him if this is true."
Rebecca:	Pause…"This is right. It was the basic garment. He had others but this was the basic one".

Note: I subsequently mentioned this information in one of my classes. A few days later one of my students brought me copy of some pages from a book called <u>City of God</u> written about 1620, and translated from the original authorized Spanish Edition by Fiscar Marison in 1902. Verse 691 says:

"In order to clothe the divine Infant in the small tunic and put on his feet the sandals made by Her, the most prudent Lady cast Herself on her knees before her sweetest Son and addressed Him in the following words: "Most high Lord, and Creator of heaven and earth, I would wish to clothe Thee, if possible, in such a way as thy Divinity deserves and I would gladly have made these garments, which are to cover Thee, from my heart-blood but I know that the poor and insignificant coverings I now offer Thee according to thy desires. Pardon me, my Lord and Master, my faults and accept the loving affection of her, who is but dust and ashes; allow me to clothe Thee." The Infant Jesus was pleased with the loving service of his purest Mother and thereupon She clothed and shod Him, setting Him upon his feet. The tunic fitted Him perfectly, covering his feet without hindering them in walking, and the sleeves extended to the middle of his hands, although She had taken no measure beforehand. The collar was cut out round, without being open in front, and was somewhat raised around the neck adjusting itself to the throat. Through this opening the heavenly Mother passed it over the head of the Infant for the garment gracefully adjusted itself according to her wishes. HE NEVER DIVESTED HIMSELF OF THIS TUNIC UNTIL THE EXECUTIONERS THEMSELVES TORE IT OFF TO SCOURGE AND AFTERWARDS CRUCIFY HIM FOR THIS GARMENT CONTINUALLY GREW WITH HIM, ADJUSTING ITSELF TO HIS BODY. The same happened also with the sandals and with the undergarment, which the solicitous Mother made for Him. None of all these articles of clothing wore away or became old in the thirty-two years, nor did the tunic lose its color or its newness, but remained just as it had left the hands of the great Lady; nor did any of them become soiled or filthy, but they preserved their first cleanliness. The garment which the redeemer of the world laid aside in order to wash the feet of his Apostles, was a mantle or cape, which He wore over his shoulders; and this also had been made by the Virgin after they had returned to Nazareth". LIKE THE OTHER CLOTHING IT GREW WITH THE LORD, WAS OF THE SAME COLOR, ONLY A LITTLE DARKER AND WAS WOVEN THE SAME WAY (emphasis mine). (591-92)

Me:	"Ask your Teacher if He can give me some advice that will help guide me in my life?"
Rebecca:	Pause…"Do as you are now except put more spirit into it and believe more than you do."
Me:	"I know this is my problem but my wife has so much fear about what I'm doing and apparently does not want me to work in this particular field and shows so much opposition. Is there anything that will guide me concerning this problem?"
Rebecca:	Pause…"I knew what the answer to this was going to be." Pause… Laughter…"Oh! whee…Well, He says the same thing I say about this. The fact is that you're not really going to get anywhere with this hanging over you. The best thing to do is to do what you want to do and maybe she will get the point. It's sort of funny."
Me:	"Maybe she will come around to my way of thinking"?
Rebecca:	"No. She has her mind set and that's the way it's going to be."
Me:	"Then doing things my way would not be going against His teachings?"

Rebecca:	"No."
Me:	"The Christian religion, as it has been passed down to us, and the story of His (Christ's) life, is this basically true?"
Rebecca:	Pause…"Yes."
Me:	"I feel I shouldn't detain Him any longer. I appreciate this and I look forward to an opportunity to do this again."
Rebecca:	"Do you have any more questions?"
Me:	"I'm sure I will after you leave."
Rebecca:	"Well, while He's here you had better ask Him some."
Me:	"A question I forgot to ask the Leader. Should I give up looking for the woman in the mountains?"
Rebecca:	Pause…"He said that you can do what you like but this woman has her free agency and she will do what she likes, and you can take it from there. As far as we know she still refuses to have any more to do with it."
Me:	"Will He confirm my beliefs in reincarnation. Do we live many lives on earth to reach our perfection?"
Rebecca:	Pause…"Yes."
Me:	"In many religions it is taught there is a Hell and Satan, and if we sin we go to an area of torment. Does such a place exist?"
Rebecca:	Pause…."This is an interpretation. There is such a person as Satan but there is no such place as Hell the way you think it is. You have your punishment with you. You get your punishment there. You don't wait until it builds up and, when you leave your area you go to either Heaven or Hell for your glory or punishment."
Me:	"Then an experience I live in the future would not be the result of something I have done in this life?"
Rebecca:	"No, because what you do in this life you are going to be punished for in this life."
Me:	"Nothing ever carries over then?"
Rebecca:	"No. You start all over fresh every time. Just a moment please" Pause…."He says one more question and He must go."

Note: This conflicts with the concept of Karma. It also contradicts the Edgar Cayce material. I regret that I didn't pursue this more with Rebecca at the time.

Karma is generally believed to be a punishment for a past action. My understanding is that it is not a punishment, but a choice we make to place ourselves in experiences which will give us a better understanding of a past action. It is common, in this belief, for emotions to carry over from one life to another. When one understands the origin and cause of a negative emotion it is no longer offensive in the current experience.

Me:	"When a person dies and leaves the physical body is the contact with God pleasant or is the person reprimanded for his sins?"
Rebecca:	Pause...."It is a joyous time. He does counsel you. He doesn't tell you that you were wrong. He just points out your mistakes. He does this in a manner which is pleasant for you, He isn't tearing you down. This way it will help you better. Most of the time you know your mistakes, but if you don't, He will tell you. If you do know you will usually tell Him".
Me:	"Well, I guess that's all. I appreciate this and I hope other opportunities like this will be given to me."
Rebecca:	"He said He is glad that you had the opportunity, that He enjoyed this meeting very much. He hopes you will do well in everything you try. Just a minute." Pause..."He is leaving now." Pause..."Are you still there?"
Me:	"Yes. You appeared to be talking to Him quite a bit there when He was leaving and I thought you had something more to say."
Rebecca:	"He was telling me something and I had some questions for Him. He was saying that you were just like He pictured you, or something like that."
Me:	"I thought you were going to find out how Christ was nailed to the cross, through the hands or wrists. Did you do that?"
Rebecca:	"Uh huh, through the hands."
Me:	"Who told you this?"
Rebecca:	"The Leader."

Me:	"What else were you going to find out?"
Rebecca:	"Some things about my past lives."
Me:	"Did you?"
Rebecca:	"Yes. In my first life experience my name was Rhone. I didn't look to see what period of time this was. Too far, you know. I was a girl, of course, and I only lived to be twelve years old in your time. There wasn't much about that life. The next life I was a doctor and my name was Amelia".
Me:	"Do you know what country you lived in during these lives?"
Rebecca:	"No. I don't think it was in your country. I died of a disease. It was an unknown disease at the time Nobody knew what it was, and I was a doctor."
Me:	"What kind of doctor? Any particular specialty?"
Rebecca:	"No. Just to help people, under-privileged people in the hills around where I was born. There were a lot of hills and mountains. In the next experience I was a lawyer and my name was Sloan. That was my first name, Sloan, and I was a woman lawyer. This was not known too much during this time. This was in an English speaking area. I couldn't speak very much English, if any, in the other areas. In all of these three experiences I was never married. I lived to be sixty-six years old. In the last experience I was a very brilliant person in anything to do with law enforcement. That's all I found out. I didn't have time to really look into it. I tried to find out if you have another person here (Like Rebecca to Irene). The Leader said to tell you that you do have to ease your conscience, but that I couldn't tell you any more about it."
Me:	"Then he must be an intelligent and handsome person?"
Rebecca:	"I don't know." Laughter…"I might even talk to the person and not know it because He said that you did and that's all I was supposed to know. All along I thought you had somebody here because you have been able to talk to me like you have, but I wasn't sure and I wasn't going to say. I've been bugging the Leader, I picked up one of your words, and He finally said yes, that you did have somebody here and that is as far as He would go. He said

	not to ask Him anymore, so I better not."
Me:	"You were going to ask about talking to me in your language."
Rebecca:	"Still no."
Me:	"Earlier we talked about when you were Rhone. At that time you told me when you finished your journey as Rhone you went directly to the level where you are now. Does this mean that the twelve years you lived as Rhone you gained enough knowledge to……."
Rebecca:	"I know what you mean. For my age I did. Usually the first lesson you don't learn much at all. You usually go to the first stage because this first lesson is to introduce you to life."
Me:	"You mean after the first experience is when you start your progress?"
Rebecca:	"Yes, and for my age I learned enough to be in the privileged area."
Me:	"When you finished your first life and went to the privileged area, (does that mean that) if you make another experience, would you have to go down?"
Rebecca:	"Go to a different area? Yes. See the first one is just a trial. Most people go back to the privileged area to learn more for the next one, and the next one is really what you're based on, the first one having been a trial. Of course, there have been people that went to the trial that just didn't make it and have been put in lower areas. Once you have been put into a lower area, you can't go any lower. Say your trial says you go to the lowest area. You don't get any lower even if you should in the next experience. You can go higher, but usually they go to my area first, and then they go from there, because the first one is a trial to get you acquainted with everything. You're not judged the first time, not unless you absolutely don't do anything."
Me:	"When we first became acquainted I asked you if there was a Hell and Satan. You said that you had never heard of either."
Rebecca:	"No. I didn't say that. I said I didn't know either the way

you meant."

Me: "What I'm getting at, when we talked to the Teacher He indicated that there was a Satan, but no Hell."

Rebecca: "The way you meant it there's not. But there is...We call him Lucifer. Yes, there is a person but not the way you meant it."

Note The way I was taught, or understood, was that Satan rules in a fiery pit deep in the earth in a place called hell.

Me: "This Lucifer, where would he be?"

Rebecca: "In the lower area, the very lowest, and all his followers."

Me: "Is he trying to entice people from higher areas to him?"

Rebecca: "Yes, when he can. It's hard for him to make contact with anyone much higher than he is. That is why he tries to make contact with people in your area."

Me: "I see, to entice them into his area rather than to go higher?"

Rebecca: "Yes."

Me: "There is no particular name for his area except that it is the lowest area?"

Rebecca: "That's right."

Me: "Would there be people in his area who would not be his followers? Those who would have a desire to raise themselves to higher areas?"

Rebecca: "I don't know."

Me: "Are you going to be able to visit me on May 11th?"

Rebecca: "Yes."

Me: "At that time there will be many people and they will have lots of questions. Will you be willing to answer what you can?"

Rebecca: "If I can, yes. What sort of questions will they be?"

Me: "I don't know. They have questions so, in their own minds, they can be satisfied in their belief in what we are doing."

Rebecca: "I will answer anything I can."

Me: "Say that you are in an experience and you have learned

and lived with knowledge in advance of the people with you in that area. When you return to the place where you are now would it be necessary for you to stay there until these people catch up with you in the knowledge you already have?"

Rebecca: "No, because there are many people doing this. If you waited for everyone to catch up some people would be waiting for long periods. I said there are many people having experiences at the same time, and if you tried to have everyone wait until the race, or whatever you want to call it, catches up with their knowledge, you would be in a mess."

Me: "You would be advanced in a particular area, and when you came back could you still be in advance of that particular area?"

Rebecca: "Yes. That's why a lot of times in your area people are smarter than other people."

Me: "But they could choose to wait on their own, couldn't they?"

Rebecca: "Yes, but usually they don't. They have their choice of whether they want to go or wait. Yes."

Me: "We have definitely established that there is my area and your area, yours being "beyond" and is the base of all knowledge of life and its purpose?"

Rebecca: "Uh huh."

Me: "Some scientists and educated men of today refuse to accept this theory. They try to keep everything on a material or physical basis. They are saying that only a portion of the mind is ever used, that the gene that forms life contains the knowledge of ancestries, and by the medium of hypnotic regression we are only awakening, through some sort of impulse, the means to release this expression of past lives. That what we are getting is only the memory factors from these cells rather then an actual contact with the 'beyond' area. What do you think about this?"

Rebecca: "I think they are all kooks."

Me: "How does a person go about proving to these people who think they know everything, that such a thing as this does exist?"

Rebecca: "You can't. They have to find out for themselves. Even if you proved it to them they wouldn't believe it. The only way they would believe it is to find out for themselves."

Me: "Then the only people who are going to find out for themselves are people who are apparently privileged, worthy, or believe it in the first place?"

Rebecca: "Usually, like saying you can't teach an old dog new tricks. That's the way it is. Once they have their minds set you can seldom ever sway them, even if you give them proof."

Me: "I'm going to have to leave. We will get together on May 11th, okay?"

Rebecca: "All right, good bye."

In October of 1991 a family of five came to my office to talk about Hypnotism. They were husband & wife, their two children and grandmother. While there they each experienced the process of hypnosis. During a session with the eighty-two year old grandmother she regressed to a past life where she identified herself as Mary Magdalene, a follower of Jesus Christ. She said that since that life experience she had not followed the teaching of the Master. In May of 1992 she returned alone to evaluate a problem with her right knee and some lumps on her arms. She also said her family was not in agreement with her experience of being with Christ so she wanted to experience that awareness again.

During this session she was directed to regress to her life with Jesus and describe her awareness. She said she was kneeling at the feet of Jesus and He was healing her. He had his left hand on her right shoulder and his right hand on her head, saying, "Arise my daughter and behold. You are purified, go among the people and be humble and helpful". I then gave her a time for silent conversation with this presence. She was told she was in perfect health, that the lumps a other conditions of the body were incidental, to live each day as it comes. She had been given answers to all her questions. She did not reveal them to me, except, when she asked to be taken from this life soon, she was told that when she was to be taken it would be up to the Father.

Chapter Eleven
CONFIRMING MY VISITS WITH THE LEADER

The regression of May 25, 1965, with the Teacher was recorded on tape as was my regression visit with Rebecca and the Leader. Only my subject, Irene, and her mother were present at these regressions. From the time of those regressions, to the present, these experiences and the information given were kept somewhat secret. Only a few close friends have since heard these tapes. I did not make public this experience until May of 1996.

It was in June of 1966, that Ken, a friend of mine who had been doing some work in hypnosis, told me he had regressed a young girl into the spiritual realm. She indicated she was on a high plane near God. She also told him that if she didn't know the answer to his questions she could ask God for the information and this would help her to learn.

When Ken told me this, I immediately saw an opportunity to confirm the truth of my regression visits with the Teacher and the Leader. Without giving him any information, or reason, I asked if he would do another regression with his subject and have her ask God if He had ever spoken to Al Ward. That was all. No explanation or purpose was offered. I had never seen or heard of the girl he had spoken of and she did not know me. Ken said this girl did not know the meaning of regression until she had been told during her first experience with hypnotism. She informed him that she was an atheist and did not believe in what regression had to offer prior to her own hypnotic experience.

Ken called on September 6, 1966, and said he had an answer to my question. In another regression his client had returned an answer that gave him quite a shock. He thought I should know about the experience and arranged to bring his taped material to my home that evening. He arrived at the appointed time accompanied by the girl whose regression had brought about this meeting.

We did a review of his taped material and I then did my own regression with the girl. The purpose was to evaluate the information she had offered about the question of my talking to God. The following is a portion of the session recorded by Ken, and some of the information given in my regression with the subject.

Ken began his regression by directing her to go into the spiritual realm to a time just prior to birth in her present life. His interview began:

Ken: "Hi, how are you?"

Girl: "Just fine."

Ken: "We haven't talked for quite a while."

Girl: "No. It's been a long time."

Ken: "Remember the last time we talked? I asked to do something for me."

Girl: "You asked me to ask God a question. You asked me to ask God if Al Ward had ever spoken God."

Ken: "Uh huh."

Girl: "Yes, he has."

Ken: "Did He tell you any more about it?"

Girl: "He said that Al was also a very wise man and a great leader of people, that he works with people's minds and tries to guide them in the path of righteousness."

Ken: "Is there anything else you can tell me?"

Girl: "Well, I'm going to be born tomorrow and I'm getting scared."

Ken: "You'll have no problem. You'll be all right."

Girl: "I'm sure I will."

Ken: "Will you be able to speak to God anymore?"

Girl: "I won't talk personally to Him anymore but He says I can come to him anytime."

We ended Ken's recording at this point and I prepared to do my own regression with his subject. She was hypnotized and directed to a time prior to birth in this life.

Me: "Tell me where you are."

Girl: "I'm in heaven."

Me: "What are you doing?"

Girl: "I'm resting."

Me: "Is there anyone with you?"

Girl:	"No, I am by myself."
Me:	"Will you describe yourself?"
Girl:	"I am dressed in a white garment and sandals. My hair hangs down straight, very long, very pretty."
Me:	"How long have you been where you are?"
Girl:	"I don't know. I don't really know."
Me:	"Do you know who you are talking to?"
Girl:	"No, I don't."
Me:	"Have you ever talked to me before?"
Girl:	"No, I haven't."
Me:	"Do you wonder why we are talking?"
Girl:	"Yes, I do."
Me:	"Do you enjoy talking to me?"
Girl:	"Yes, I do."

Note: In a regression, with another person, the subject had said, "I enjoy talking to you because you force me to reach further up to get answers which I would not do otherwise. It's very hard for us to grow by ourselves. We need the energy that you bring us to help us. Of course, we are able to do things that you can't that we need. We need your energy. I get a real good feeling talking to you."

Me:	"Do you know where I am?"
Girl:	"No, I don't."
Me:	"Do you think I am where you are, or somewhere else?"
Girl:	"You're somewhere else."
Me:	"How do you know this?"
Girl:	"Because you speak and people here do not speak."
Me:	"How do they communicate?"
Girl:	"It's vibrations."
Me:	"Do you know what plane or level you're on?"
Girl:	"Very high, very high level."
Me:	"Do you know of higher levels than where you are?"
Girl:	"The level of birth."

Me: "What about the level of creation?"

Girl: "Yes. That's where I am."

Me: "Do you have people there who rule or guide you?"

Girl: "Yes. We have leaders."

Me: "What is the name of the highest leader?"

Girl: "The highest leader? Our Lord Jesus."

Me: "Is there no one higher than Him?"

Girl: "God."

Me: "How would you describe God?"

Girl: "Very beautiful."

Me: "As an individual?"

Girl: "Yes. A very beautiful man."

Me: "What about Christ?"

Girl: "Also very pretty."

Me: "Can you make a comparison of their appearances?"

Girl: "God is older and just beams in radiance, so much radiance. Jesus is much younger."

Me: "Is there anything you want to talk to me about?"

Girl: "Yes, there is. Are you in the same place, a place called Earth as Ken is?"

Me: "Yes."

Girl: "That's what I thought. Are you Al?"

Me: "Yes."

Girl: "You're the man I asked God about?"

Me: "That's right. When you asked that question what was His response?"

Girl: "God just told me that you were a very wise man. You help others and you have the power to rule, or overcome, a person's mind and that you use this power very well."

Me: "What about Jesus? Are you able to talk to Him, also?"

Girl: "I don't talk to Him. I just talk to God."

Me: "What's the reason for this?"

Girl: "I don't know. I really don't know. God is there all the time."

Me:	"What is your opinion of being able to have this conversation with me?"
Girl:	"I don't know. I really don't know. It's nice. I enjoy it."
Me:	"Does talking with me give you a desire to accomplish anything?"
Girl:	"It gives me the desire that I want to be born again. I didn't want to be born."
Me:	"In being born again, have you selected any particular type of experience?"
Girl:	"No. God places us where He feels we are most needed."
Me:	"You say born again. Does this mean you have lived other experiences?"
Girl:	"Yes, I have. I believe I have once."
Me:	"Have you ever heard of the word reincarnation?"
Girl:	"No."
Me:	"Have you ever heard of the word re-cycle?"
Girl:	"No, I haven't"
Me:	"Life experiences?"
Girl:	"Yes."
Me:	"What is the meaning of life experiences?"
Girl:	"It's things you experienced in a past life and you overcome in a new life."
Me:	"What is the reason for these life experiences?"
Girl:	"Just knowledge. I think it's just knowledge."
Me:	"Where does this all lead to?"
Girl:	"The fulfillment of life. It's all in fulfillment."
Me:	"What happens when you have this fulfillment? Where do you go then?"
Girl:	"You're supposed to be prepared again to go to God."
Me:	"When you go to God, is this a reference to everlasting life?"
Girl:	"Yes. It's life forever and ever. There's no end."
Me:	"Is that in your area or where I am?"
Girl:	"Where you are and where I am."

Me:	"I don't understand how this can be. Do you have an explanation?"
Girl:	"Yes, I do. You have birth and you have death. Death is the same as being born and birth is the same as death."
Me:	"Why then the different areas?"
Girl:	"I don't know this."
Me:	"What about the people who have lived and died? Are they here on earth or where?"
Girl:	"Yes, they are on earth. They are also here."
Me:	"Can they be at both places at the same time?"
Girl:	"No."
Me:	"Where does this separation come in?"
Girl:	"Through death."
Me:	"The way we understand it here is that when a person dies he is placed in the ground and…"
Girl:	"The body, but not the Soul."
Me:	"What happens to the Soul?"
Girl:	"The Soul just rises and comes to my area and is formed into a person."
Me:	"What is the purpose in the area where you are? Would you say it is re-education?"
Girl:	"Yes, to overcome some of your wrong doings, to overcome fears and sins, things like that."
Me:	"When you are in the beyond area are you more aware of what your fears, sins, and wrong doings have been in my area?"
Girl:	"Yes, Yes, definitely."
Me:	"Then this would be an aid in helping you to understand and overcome these things when you come into a new life experience?"
Girl:	"Yes."
Me:	"Are there levels other than yours?"
Girl:	"Yes, there are."
Me:	"Why the separation of levels?"
Girl:	"God raises you to levels according to how your feelings are.

When I first came here I was at a very low level, very dark. I didn't want to be born. As each day passed and I spoke to God, just speaking to Him made me see the reason I should be born again. Each time of speaking to Him I was raised to a new level. At each level, I went it was a little lighter; now I'm here."

Me: "In other words, you can raise yourself to higher levels without making an experience on earth?"

Girl: "Yes, or you can stay at a level."

Me: "Do you have any idea of the level I have obtained?"

Girl: "Very high, very high level."

Me: "Why do you say this?"

Girl: "Because you have the power to be up here with God and also be on earth."

Me: "You said you didn't know me, you have never spoken to me before. How do you know this?"

Girl: "Because God told me this when I spoke to Him about you."

Me: "Is there anything else you want to talk about?"

Girl: "When I am born, will I be wise like you?"

Me: "That depends on whether you apply the knowledge and wisdom you have learned there. This word "wise" means what?

Girl: "Intelligence, power, just everything."

Me: "To obtain a higher level, does this have anything to do with knowledge of material things or is it strictly knowledge of life?"

Girl: "Knowledge of life."

Me: "How are you informed in your lessons?"

Girl: "Just by what God tells us. It's vibrations, and He speaks with us."

Me: "How would you explain a vibration?"

Girl: "Just like a pitch, a tone, a pitch."

This ended our regression. I have not seen or heard from Ken or this girl since. Because of the responses I received from regressions I became anxious to obtain the opinions of others concerning the validity of this information.

Thirty people, including two professors from a nearby university, were selected to attend a meeting with Irene/Rebecca on May 11, 1965. The two professors each provided me with a list of questions they had prepared. The guests were encouraged to ask any questions on any subject and to question or challenge any answers that did not satisfy them. I had asked many of the questions in other regressions but they were asked again for the satisfaction of those in attendance.

Because of the large number of people at this meeting this regression turned out to be the longest visit I had with Rebecca. Although it resulted in many questions being answered I do not consider it as important as some of my other sessions. Even after being able to question any response from Rebecca the people in the group still refused to believe what they had seen and experienced. Although they received answers to their questions many would not accept the validity, or the value, of the regression process. It seems their previous beliefs were challenged when God was described as an individual. They preferred the concept that God is spirit.

I realize each individual will, or will not, believe according to his own understanding. Each person must find and prove God for himself. It is the desire, belief, faith, and confidence of the hypnotic subject, and the hypnotist, that makes possible a type of contact with the spirit, soul, or God-part of our being. The things my subjects say are no different from those being hypnotically regressed by others. An individual may experience something different in the way certain knowledge is revealed. I seemed to have experienced something different in the regressions where contact was made with the Leader and Teacher. These experiences were given to me as a learning process. I was told no one else had experienced this in the same manner. Rebecca indicated this was an experiment by the Leader to prove that knowledge can be communicated in this way. However, everyone has the potential to reveal different and important information through this process.

Every person I have ever hypnotized and regressed has described a pre-natal awareness to their present life. I have learned that each and every human being has within their deeper consciousness a spiritual awareness and an association with the spiritual realm at his level of accomplishment. Hypnotism, which is far from being the only means of communication, is one way in which this God-part can be experienced.

To my knowledge it has never been satisfactorily determined as to what makes one person, over another, more responsive to this type of communication with the spirit world. My own opinion is that it has something to do with one's nature as it relates to true spiritual awareness or true spiritual growth and level.

The following is the personal testimony of a person who experienced hypnosis for the first time for the reason of self-improvement. It is typical of the response by those who have opened their minds to the spiritual awareness within themselves. It was of her own choice that she gave me this testimony entitled "What Hypnosis Means To Me".

As in all professions, such as medicine, law, the Church, etc, we find the good and bad. Also in the rank of hypnotists we find those who play at it and those who truly attempt to fathom the depths of the unknown. In my estimation, the true hypnotist ranks among the highest. He then becomes another Christ in manifestation being about his Father's business. He has at his disposal the very power to perform so-called miracles, depending on the degree or intensity of his faith and belief in himself. In order to accomplish this, I feel that he must be a truly spiritual person, becoming a channel through which he performs all his work from the sacred temple of his being. Knowing this, he works in a realm that is higher than the physical. He comes in contact with the Real, a realm of complete awe and reverence.

On the other hand, I feel that the subject, in order to derive all the good that is given, must likewise be spiritually attuned. It is my belief that if one realizes what is taking place and has complete faith and confidence in the hypnotist, that anything can take place. Of course, one must realize that here too, there are degrees of attainment, and so a great deal depends on the attunement of the hypnotist and the subject. One will receive only as much as he is capable of receiving. As the hypnotist proceeds to put the subject to sleep, he (the subject) feels himself leaving the material world. He seems to lose all sense of self-consciousness and is no longer aware of his immediate environment. The only thing that matters is the voice of the hypnotist, hence my belief in a spiritual attunement, faith and confidence. The hypnotist is now using a higher power that rises above the mere physical. As Jesus said, "It is not I, but the Father working through me". The subject now drifts slowly to the part of the self that is the real center of the person. He is no longer conscious of any worries, fears, frustration, illness, lack, or any obstacle. His whole being is quiet, still. The subject is completely unaware of the physical or those about him, except the voice of the hypnotist. He is now in a realm where anything can take place. It is here that the true hypnotist, a master of men, uses himself as a channel or means through which this power, or God, acts through him. He is at the controls, you could say, of a great time machine of which he pulls the levers. At that moment he is performing the miracle of the "Eternal Now." He can take the subject to the past, present, or even the future. (Some suggestions given are, at times, accomplished after the subject awakens and can last for days, weeks, or even months, again depending upon the degree of intensity.) Past present, or future, however, does take place in the "Eternal Now." The hypnotist has but to pull the lever and the only feeling his subject will have is "Now".

I would compare this experience to seeing the whole instead of a part as we do in the physical. Time means nothing and is nothing in that realm of consciousness. Again, it can be compared to a dream. So much can happen in just a flash. Here the hypnotist can, again depending on his and the subject's faith, change a physical handicap to become the Real, which is always perfect and whole. He can make the blind see, the deaf hear and the dumb speak. He can make someone whole again. He can, in so many words, raise the dead, the untrue in us, to life, real life. He can make his subject feel the true, the beautiful, the unblemished in its state of perfection. In other words, he can give us back life and when we awaken, it is up to us to keep this life flowing by tasting of its pure Essence in the "Eternal Now." When one awakens, or is brought back, the feeling remains; the subject feels wonderful, revitalized. It is as if the hand of God has touched him and assured him that all is well. We must learn to listen to our subconscious, our inner selves but alas, we have so much to overcome when operating through our physical or self-conscious selves. On this plane we allow our five physical senses to take over and it is then that the refreshing waters of the subconscious are dammed up by a million and one thoughts of the material. I feel that through hypnosis we are given the opportunity to train the spiritual. I believe that through repetition and constant use of this gift we eventually can learn to evaluate the true from the unreal. I have the deepest respect, gratitude and reverence for this great power and the individual who is endowed with this great gift. My only prayer is that others can come to appreciate it and to experience the riches and wonders of it as I have.

Chapter Twelve
REBECCA'S LAST CONTACT

She Brings A Friend

A regression was arranged with my subject, Irene. A few other people were in attendance. One of those present was a psychic medium. She and my brother Richard were the only ones Rebecca was able to hear and talk to during my regressions with Irene. This regression started as usual with the question, "Rebecca, how have you been?"

Rebecca:	"Fine, How have you been?"
Me:	"I have been having quite a time since our last visit. Nobody wants to believe me when I tell them about talking to God."
Rebecca:	"Well, what have you done to have them believe you?"
Me:	"I'm working on it. We have a few other people here tonight taking part in this experience."
Rebecca:	"Yes, I know. I feel that one person who is with you is very close to me. I feel a bright light, a warm light in my presence I have never felt before."
Me:	"You're right. This lady has demonstrated her psychic abilities to me."
Rebecca:	"Uh huh, yes. She is very gifted and very privileged or she wouldn't be able to do what she does."
Me:	"Would it be possible for her to talk to you and ask questions?"
Rebecca:	"You mean not going through you. I don't know if I can or not. She can try."
Psychic:	"Do I tell the truth when I say that I see Christ?"
Me:	"Did you hear that?"
Rebecca:	"Yes. I imagine she does tell the truth. I'm not doubting her word. There are a lot of people who see Him. A lot of people say, who does that person think he is?"
Me:	"You mean like me. Who do I think I am to be able to talk

	to God? Why should this happen to me?"
Rebecca:	"Well, in your book, what do you call it, the Bible? He talked to people just like I talk to you. So why shouldn't He be able to do it now? There are more years but it doesn't change the person. Twenty years from now you're going to be the same person. You might have a different outlook, but you're still the same person as a whole. Also, people put Him so far ahead of them, put Him on a pedestal so far above them, they can't comprehend Him lowering to the same level they are."
Me:	"Am I to understand that souls, or those in your realm, have a good contact with people in my area even though we are not aware of this?"
Rebecca:	"Oh yes. They are there all the time. You can't see them but they are around. Let me give you an example. I have a good friend here. He said one day he was with his mother and she was upset about something and started to walk out into the street. A car came by and she looked up just in time to move. What happened is that he told her mind, or what ever you want to call it, to look up but she didn't know this. She thought she did it on her own, but see, this way he helped her, so they are always around."
Me:	"Don't some people have the ability to see them?"
Rebecca:	"Oh yes."
Me:	"Many people, and religions, recognize Christ as an individual, but look upon God as energy."
Rebecca:	"Yes. They can't comprehend it because Christ came to Earth and there are records of this. People are going to believe this more. God didn't do like Christ did so it is going to be harder for people to understand."

My two years of doing hypnotic regressions with sixteen year old Irene resulted in several exciting experiences. My visits with the Leader and Teacher, Rebecca's travels through different spiritual levels, and preparing for a new physical incarnation will always be remembered. Several times I asked Rebecca if I could communicate with others in her realm only to be told it was not possible at the time. She prepared me for the time that I would no longer be able to contact her. She gave the date of her departure as June 18, 1965. On this date I had my last regression with Irene and contact with Rebecca. Shortly afterwards Irene and her family moved to Texas. We began our session in the usual manner.

Me:	"Rebecca, what are you doing?"
Rebecca:	"Waiting for you."
Me:	"What are we going to talk about today?"
Rebecca:	"I have a friend with me. He won't be able to stay too long. He has a meeting to go to. He says he will stay as long as he can."
Me:	"Is your friend specialized in any expression we can talk about? Describe him to me."
Rebecca:	"He has dark hair, medium height, 180 pounds, and his name is Raca."
Me:	"Then you suggest we talk with him first?"
Rebecca:	"Yes."
Me:	"What is his opinion about what we have been doing?"
Rebecca:	Pause…"He said it's wonderful. He wishes he had known about it sooner so he could have been here more times."
Me:	"Does he know how this is done?"
Rebecca:	"Through a person. Yes, I told him."
Me:	"I mean the procedure. Would he have any advice on how to accomplish more in this expression?"
Rebecca:	Pause…"He says the only thing he can suggest is that you study and do it as often as you can."
Me:	"Can I become advanced enough for people in your area to contact me?"
Rebecca:	Pause… "Yes."
Me:	"This is difficult. I wasn't expecting this."
Rebecca:	"You asked me to bring someone."
Me:	"What are his main duties there?"
Rebecca:	Pause…"His duties for your level is to help. His duty here is he's the master of his house with two other males. If either of them decides something he has to approve it. He takes care of their needs."
Me:	"What significance does he place on my talking to the

	Leader and Teacher?"
Rebecca:	Pause... "You must be very privileged."
Me:	"Do either of you have any knowledge of what we call the third eye?"
Rebecca:	Pause..."I don't. He doesn't remember anything."
Me:	"It's a sixth sense, the power to see outside of the five senses."
Rebecca:	"Oh."
Me:	"Does he desire to go on a mission to my area?"
Rebecca:	Pause... "Not at this time he doesn't."
Me:	"Does he have any questions for me?"
Rebecca:	Pause... "He wants to know everything about your teachings. Go slow. I have to tell him."
Me:	"The basis of my teaching is to show other people the powers of their own minds so they can understand themselves and others better and to have more awareness of their existence in your area."
Rebecca:	"He says that is a good explanation."
Me:	"Demonstrations and explaining hypnotism helps them understand better."
Rebecca:	Pause..."He wants to know exactly how you do it. Go through the routine of putting your teaching into practice. This way he can better understand."
Me:	"By using a set of words to bring about a state of concentration to call up things which exist in the Soul."
Rebecca:	"He wants to know how you relate the subconscious mind to the Soul."
Me:	"The conscious mind is what we do. The subconscious mind is what we are. The Soul is God or the link between this area and your area. Is that what he means?"
Rebecca:	"Very good, he says. Just a minute." Pause... "What happens if a person wants to be hypnotized and then decides he doesn't. After he is under, can a person come out? He doesn't see how this will help if the person is afraid."
Me:	"This procedure involves the desire of both the hypnotist

	and subject. Psychologically you can get a subject to react against his desire. But this is a part of my teaching: to inform my subjects to decide for themselves what they want to respond to."
Rebecca:	"Can you do this to more than one person at a time?"
Me:	"Yes. However, each person is responding to the hypnotist independently."
Rebecca:	"To change the subject a little bit. He wants to know has this ever been used as a weapon?"
Me:	"This method has been known by many other names such as brainwashing. It has been and is being used in the same sense as a weapon."
Rebecca:	"He says wouldn't people in your area be scared of it?"
Me:	"They are. People have been so misled and have so little knowledge of this art that it makes them afraid. This again relates to my teaching in which I try to show people that this is something that can't be forced on them if they understand it properly."
Rebecca:	"Is this why you are writing books?"
Me:	"Yes. To give the people a better understanding of these forces they have within themselves so they can use it to better themselves."
Rebecca:	Pause…"He doesn't see where this is going to really help. If people are afraid, they wouldn't be reading books about it."
Me:	"It isn't that everybody is afraid of it. It's only a misunderstanding of it. If they have a better understanding others do not have the power to use it as a weapon against them."
Rebecca:	Pause… "Yes, he understands." Pause… "Is it true you can do this to yourself?"
Me:	"Yes. We call it self-hypnosis. This is also a part of my teaching. What a hypnotist can help or cause people to do by using the powers of their own mind they can accomplish the same by their own ability."
Rebecca:	Pause…"How do you bring yourself out?"
Me:	"The sub-conscious never sleeps. It's like a twilight sleep.

	What you can do with the mind you can undo. Has Raca ever been contacted?" ·
Rebecca:	Pause… "Not in this way."
Me:	"What does he do for entertainment?"
Rebecca:	Pause…"Long walks, talks, and just being together."
Me:	"Does he talk about women?"
Rebecca:	Pause…Laughter… "That's usually the subject. Females are usually present."
Me:	"What is Raca's opinion of the female's place in my area?"
Rebecca:	"What he thinks?" Pause…"The way he thinks it should be doesn't mean that's the way it is. He thinks females should be servants to men. They should do all the things women are to do and everything he asks them to do."
Me:	"Well, what's wrong with that? That's what Robert had to say. The man is the master and the woman is the slave. That's the way it was in the beginning and that's the way it will be in the end."
Rebecca:	"Not if I have anything to do with it. I agree that men should be the masters but they should not take advantage."
Me:	"Do you understand juvenile delinquency? What can you and your friend advise to improve this situation?"
Rebecca:	"This may take a minute." Pause… "We both agree that you can't be too lenient on children and you can't be too strict. You have to hit a happy medium. Usually delinquents are allowed to run like they want to and a lot don't have much to do. This gets them into trouble. If parents and people would give them something to do this would cut down delinquency considerably. You have to start when the children are very young, to raise them to know what is right and wrong."
Me:	"Between five and nine?"
Rebecca:	"As soon as they start knowing, understanding, and for the rest of their lives."
Me:	"Is there such a thing as an original sin? A sin that a person is born with?"
Rebecca:	Pause…"No."

Me:	"What about baptism? Can we enter into heaven without being baptized?"
Rebecca:	"No, it's mandatory. The Teacher was baptized."
Me:	"What's the purpose?"
Rebecca:	"I don't know, let's see." Pause… "We think it symbolizes washing away sins. Of course one can sin afterwards, but it should be done at least once."
Me:	"What happens to one who is not baptized?"
Rebecca:	"Never gets to the highest level. It depends on the circumstance. Like children from birth to about twelve: if they haven't been baptized you can't judge them. One who knows what to do and not to do—this is taken into consideration."
Me:	"What about confession? Can you wash away your sins by confession?"
Rebecca:	Pause…"To the Leader, yes."
Me:	"What about confessing your sins to a priest?"
Rebecca:	"A person? No. Because this person is human. In the Book of The Leader the idea is that if you want to be forgiven of your sins you have to speak them unto the Leader (God). It doesn't mention going through a person who can sin as much as you can."
Me:	"Why do we have so many different languages?"
Rebecca:	Pause…"I don't know, but Raca said this is a process of learning.
Me:	"Why exactly did the Teacher (Christ) come to earth?"
Rebecca:	Pause… "To give people in your area life, everlasting life."
Me:	"What did Christ mean when he said, 'You will do greater things than I'"?
Rebecca:	"Probably things invented. He didn't mean you could walk on water, etc. No one ever heard of electricity. Just a minute." Pause… "He agrees. He doesn't want to be left out of anything."
Me:	"Does a priest have the right to refuse to baptize a child because of a parent's sin?"

Rebecca:	"No."
Me:	"Does a marriage have to be sanctioned by the church to be accepted by God?"
Rebecca:	"No."
Me:	"What makes a marriage?"
Rebecca:	Pause…"If it's done in the Leader's name. It's a holy union and should be done in God's name."
Me:	"No third party?"
Rebecca:	"It should be done by someone with knowledge and authority."
Me:	"Does Raca have any more questions?"
Rebecca:	Pause… "No. He has to go now. He really enjoyed it and wishes he had more opportunities to talk with you."
Me:	"How do we say good-bye? Are you going to cry when I'm gone?"
Rebecca:	"No. Good-bye."

Chapter Thirteen
SPECIAL CASES

THE CASE OF ROSEMARY/DENOTICA

All her life Rosemary thought she was from another planet. She was a young lady, aged 23, with no more than a high school education who was planning to study cosmetology and work in a beauty salon. In 1979, she came to the Parks Research and Education Project (PREP) with a physical problem. This was her first experience with hypnotism and age regression. During the evaluation of her infirmity a personality change occurred. Rosemary was now Denotica, who said she was communicating with me from another planet called Valynta, eighty-nine light years from Earth. She said it would take five hundred years for us to reach her planet by our present maximum speed of travel. Later on checking with an astronomer I learned that a light year is six trillion miles and the closest galaxy to earth is one hundred seventy light years away.

A follow-up session was scheduled to evaluate the responses of the first session. When Denotica was contacted at this session her words were broken and the sentences were incomplete, similar to static on a radio. I stopped the session and questioned Rosemary about what was happening and why her words were incomplete. She stated that during the time I was trying to communicate with Denotica she felt as if her entire body was bloating, getting bigger and bigger. When asked how she felt after being brought out of hypnosis, she assured me that she felt fine. At another session, a week later, I asked Denotica what had happened during the previous session and she said, "The frequency was not right. If you had continued there would have been an explosion."

At one of our sessions Denotica asked if I would like to talk with her leader. (Remember Rebecca had asked me this same question when I was working with Irene thirteen years earlier.) When this occurred Rosemary, who was a small, frail 23-year-old, lay on my couch responding to my directions. Denotica identified her leader as Modar. She said I would have to call him out. By this she meant I would have to communicate on a compatible frequency by speaking to him first. While this was happening Rosemary's neck swelled to twice its normal size, her voice became deep, and she spoke in a different language. In a few moments Denotica advised me that Modar was using both the male and female voice boxes simultaneously, in his own language. The attempt to communicate with Modar had to be terminated.

Denotica described herself as a typical alien with silvery skin, immense eyes, small mouth, no nose bridge, only openings above her mouth, long arms and no hair. I asked if her people considered her beautiful, and she said, "All is beautiful that does not hurt." Although Denotica said Modar was the leader of her planet she also said there is only one God over all. Each system has its own commandments; some are called Lentons, some Ramatas, and some just the Ten Rules.

One day in 1998, I was working with another woman. During the session I asked if she had ever heard of any of these terms. When I mentioned Ramatas her whole body shook. After the session I asked if she ever felt alien to her environment and she said she had always felt different and that perhaps she was alien to the earth system.

One day Rosemary called to say she had been talking to a man about her regression experience and he told her to read The Uranita Book. She found this book in the public library and, after reading it, felt she was one of the people in the book. The book mentions, "Thought Adjusters," "Divine Builders," "Energy Manipulators," and "Workers" as spirit entities from another solar system who assist in helping earth life evolve. The Uranita Book is 2,097 pages in length and gives a detailed description of the nature of God and the creation and structure of both Earth and the Universe. This information is purported to have been channeled from spirit entities. Both Rosemary and I believe she is one of these channels. This fascinating book is published by the Urantia Foundation in Chicago, Illinois.

I used Rosemary to demonstrate hypnotic age regression to a class of 15 to 20 people which I was conducting. The class was allowed to ask questions on any subject. A woman present told of one of her daughters dying of cancer at age twelve and wanted Denotica to tell her why this would happen to such a young person. Denotica told her the girl had a bad seed. A gene, passed to her from one of her parents lay dormant in her body until age twelve when it became active, causing the problem. The woman said her doctor had told her the same thing. Her husband had been hospitalized for a genetic problem.

Denotica went on to describe other medical problems. She said blindness is sometimes caused by a coating forming on the optic nerve and at the present time this coating cannot be removed without severing the affected nerve and causing total permanent blindness. In the future we will develop an instrument which will be able to remove this coating and restore sight. We now have, or are developing, the laser which will do this job. She further stated that cancers will be treated by low-voltage electricity of the same frequency we have in our bodies. She said the procedures we have now not only kill the cancer cells but also kill the good cells as well. Low-voltage electricity is not intended to kill the cancer cells but rather to separate them and render them harmless. Denotica also told me how to place a person on a metal table (or something compatible to aluminum foil) and by Joining hands with six other "believers", we could mentally draw the illness out of the sick body.

We also talked about the reality of UFO's, Big Foot, and the existence of vortexes, which allow fast space travel between planets and systems without protective coverings. Her response to all of these was simply "Yes, they are real. Just because you haven't seen them doesn't mean they are not real."

At one of our sessions Rosemary was regressed to a recent past life where she identified herself as Bonnie Parker of the infamous Bonnie and Clyde pair. When she started to tell me about her life I suggested there were many books, movies and other extensive information about her life. I asked her to tell me something about herself that only she knew.

She told me that as a young girl her mother had given her an heirloom necklace that had been in their family for generations. Her mother told her she was never to sell, give away, or lose this necklace but to pass it on to her children. For safekeeping she had buried it under a tree in the front yard of their home. She gave me the name of a town in Missouri, her home address, and where to stand on the front porch of their home to identify the tree where the necklace was buried.

THE BENTWATERS CASE

About ten years ago I received a phone call from a movie producer in Los Angeles who had heard about my work in hypnosis. He interviewed me for almost an hour, thoroughly checking my credentials. He said he had contact with an ex-military airman who had experienced a UFO incident in 1980, while stationed in England. The airman felt he wanted to talk about the incident but could not remember the details. The producer was looking for a hypnotist who could recover this information.

Arrangements were made for me to meet with the producer and the airman in Los Angeles to conduct a hypnotic regression. Under hypnosis the airman described how he and his supervisor had left the barracks in a Jeep heading to his post for guard duty. In route they noticed some strange looking lights in the forest outside the base and, on investigating, observed an odd-shaped craft with blinking lights around its center. It appeared to be pulsating and changing shape as it moved through the trees. Frightened, they returned to the base determined not to say anything about what they had experienced.

The following night, while sleeping, the airman suddenly awoke saying to himself, "They're back". He dressed and returned to the area where he had observed the craft. On his arrival he found several military personnel and civilians present watching this strange craft. The colonel in charge of the base was there taking moving pictures and directing others at the scene. This Officer told him to see how close he could get to the craft and, following orders he got to within ten feet of it when he was suddenly repelled thirty feet backwards. After a while the craft left the area at a high rate of speed. All of the military personnel at the scene were returned to base, debriefed, and told not to talk to anyone about the incident.

Following recovery of the details of this three-day incident I had my subject regress to where he had been closest to the UFO and then had him focus his attention on the lights to see if there was a personality behind them. He said, "Yes, one of the red ones does". I told him to talk to the light, to ask who or what it was and where it came from. The information given through this light was as follows. "We come from a system far from Earth. We are here. We have been here. We are in your ground, your water, and your skies. We are here to observe you because we believe we were once your form. We travel at the speed of light and stop at a base on Mars before coming to your Earth."

I asked why these beings had chosen my subject to be the one most connected to this incident. The response was, "Because of his mind. We can control it". I asked, "If you travel at the speed of light how long does it take you to get from Mars to Earth?" The response was, "One hour". I then asked if the beings knew of Denotica and Modar and the response was affirmative. So I asked, "What would you say if I told you I had talked to both of them". The reply was, "That's impossible". When I asked if they wanted to talk to me about it, I was told, "No, we are not interested in you".

During the time of this communication we observed a red streak about an inch wide on the neck of my subject. The red streak came from below his shirt collar and went up and over both his ears. When the communication was over and I moved the man to another awareness these red streaks vanished. He had been unaware of these marks and felt no unusual sensations.

About a week after this session the producer called to say he had computed the time and distance between Earth and Mars and had determined that, at the speed of light, it would take 46 minutes to make the trip. Taking into account acceleration and deceleration to and from the speed of light, one hour would be about the right amount of time.

I had been asked by the producer not to talk about this session but, since the incident has been well documented, I see no harm, at this point, in identifying how the information was recovered. The details of this incident have been presented in several television programs. The Discovery Channel aired this incident on January 11, 1998. In my opinion this was the most accurate presentation according to what was recovered through hypnosis. The incident has become known as, "The Bentwaters Case," since it occurred near the NATO Bases of the RAF Woodridge and RAF Bentwaters in December of 1980. These bases were on lease to the US Air force at the time of the incident.

Personally I have never seen an Alien or their Crafts, but I have worked with many who have had these personal experiences. Jim Marrs reported this incident in his book, "The Alien Agenda". In 1982 Brenda Butler, in London, England, covered the same incident in her book, "Sky Crash, A Cosmic Conspiracy".

Talking about UFO's. In June of 1993 a twenty-six year old man came to my office to see if hypnosis could refresh his memory. He said when he was sixteen he and his three brothers observed a UFO while living on an air base in Nevada. Recently he had been having frightening dreams about the incident but was unable to remember the details. He told that his father was in the Air force and they were living in a housing tract on the base. One day he and his brothers climbed a fence to a restricted area of the base and started up a hill that separated the base from the housing. They all observed a flying disc landing on the hill. A non-human form came out of the UFO, waved to them, returned to the craft and departed. The boys went to a friend's home and told about the incident. Their friends thought the experience was "neat". When they went home and reported the incident to their father, they were told to "Forget It". He believes the United States Government has these things that are not of this world. He determined, in hypnosis, that his dreams indicated a fear of really knowing the truth of this incident. He said two of his brothers are indifferent to the experience and the other brother takes the attitude, "So what, we saw a UFO".

THE CASE OF DARLA

Darla had been feeling so stressed she checked herself into a hospital emergency unit on several different occasions but each time they were unable to determine the cause. A friend referred her to a woman who did acupressure and, while having this treatment, Darla went into convulsions which lasted for three hours. She was then referred to me.

During our interview Darla told me she had been the victim of alien abductions several times. The first time, at age seven, an alien had taken her from her home into a nearby forest at which time she observed her four-year-old brother in the presence of other aliens and their spacecraft. She stated that her brother has also lived a life fraught with emotional and physical problems. During one of the abductions an implant was placed in her head just behind her right ear. She believed the pressure placed on this spot during the accupressure treatment was the cause of her convulsions.

Darla said she was at first uncomfortable and frightened at being in my presence but submitted to the process of hypnosis anyway. Immediately, on entering hypnosis, she went into convulsions. I proceeded to speak calmly suggesting she could just relax and allow the convulsions to stop. Within moments she relaxed and I inquired about the origin and cause of her problem. At this time another personality within her spoke to me in a language I couldn't understand. However, I knew I was being scolded vehemently for interfering with Darla's problem. When I asked for an English translation I was told that Darla was being given extra energy to prepare her for a future event that had nothing to do with her alien abductions. I argued that she was getting too much energy for her physical system and suggested slacking off for a while until she could handle it. The entity with whom I was communicating agreed to reduce Darla's energy level as I requested. I asked this entity to give me her spiritual level and I thought she said fifteen, which I repeated. I was told, in no uncertain terms, that the level was "fifty". To my knowledge, Darla has not experienced this amount of stress, anxiety, or convulsions since that session.

A few months later, while attending one of my classes, Darla thought she recognized one of the men present in the class. Ed thought Darla also looked familiar even though, to their knowledge, they had never met. We looked behind Ed's right ear and found a scar, matching Darla's, of which he been unaware. Ed has a great interest in UFO's but refuses to consider any connection to Darla and/or aliens.

THE CASE OF CHA-CHA

About six years ago I was doing a past life regression with a lady who had displayed good psychic abilities. She told me she had come to Earth from another planet and was, at that time, one of a species which were both male and female who could reproduce offspring within themselves. The strength and beauty of Earth people thrilled her. Their mother ship had to depart Earth under emergency conditions and some of her people were not able to get aboard before it left. Those who were left behind had been placed in hibernation in capsules and buried deep in our mountains to await the return of their people. While in hibernation she decided not to wait so she died and was later born into an Earth life.

In a past life on Earth she had been a Black Foot Indian girl who had been put in charge of the animals because she could communicate with them. Following the session she said, "Well, that explains it! I can walk down any street in any city and all the animals in the neighborhood will follow me."

THE CASE OF RENATO/ROBERT

In 1956, at the time the United States launched its first space vehicle, I did a regression with my sixteen-year-old nephew Renato at which time I made contact with the spirit personality connected with him. He would not identify himself or respond to my questions. He said he didn't know me, or what I was doing and he would have to "check up on me" to find out if I was entitled to the information for which I was asking.

At our second session several days later the spirit entity gave his name as Robert. He said he had checked up on me and then asked what I wanted to know. I questioned him as to whether or not he knew of our space probe to the moon. He said yes, but that we should be going for the backside of the moon where we would find microscopic animal life, which has developed certain characteristics that make it possible to live in different climates. He went on to say the backside of the moon is so cold we wouldn't believe it. The life form he described seems to be similar to the 1997, evaluation of the microscopic life form found in the rocks from Mars. He said that we would go to the backside of the moon that human life would be lost at first, but we would eventually succeed.

During another regression Robert stated that I had interrupted him as he was preparing to go to a distant planet. I said, "Go ahead, I will talk to you later". His response was "No, It will only take a short time". In about two seconds he said, "I'm back, you can't imagine how far I went".

I asked another subject in regression if he knew of life on other planets. He said, "They tell me there are other forms and units of energies that exist, but some planets are in the process of growing and developing while others are dying out. The principles that pertain to planets are the same as those that also pertain to, and affect, us. They tell me that people on earth are thinking of going to Mars by developing something to transport their bodies. We are able to transport ourselves, or be where we want to be, by thought. They tell us we can go to other planets but we don't have to have the elements that you people must have. We have our own source of energy. Life on other planets is basically the same as yours. It's a polarity with a center and a sphere with a source of energy."

My subject Rebecca had stated that every planet has a life form. Some of them, closer to the sun, are not as high in intelligence as those of earth but they have life that carries on. Life on other planets may be in the form of vegetation or animal types rather than human form, as we know it. She said she didn't have contact with other worlds but had learned this from the Leader and Teacher. Her contact is mostly with our world.

Rebecca always referred to our Bible as "The Book of the Leader". During a regression with a male entity I asked if he knew about our Bible. He said, "Yes, I know something about it. It came about by a multiple of inspirations. A number of people in a higher realm gave these thoughts. This was done elsewhere, too, in other books, but the word kills the spirit even though the word is necessary. You see, the people who wrote these things received the spirit first and then wrote the word so it came as thoughts, then became words, and the words kill the spirit, words distort the spirit".

In another regression with Renato/Robert, I told him I had talked to a spirit entity named Rebecca. He said, "Rebecca, I know her. She's a high vibration, higher than mine is. You are very privileged to have talked to her.

If people would only realize what you are doing your name would go down in history, as you would say. If they could only know you talked to a person like that. She's a teacher but she's not the highest of them all". I told him that Rebecca said I would be able to talk to God and Christ. He said, "I'll tell you that, too, because talking to you I know you will. You'll put your mind to it and if you think about it long enough, you will. How do you think these prophets did it in ancient times? It would be kind of funny if they were lying, wouldn't it?"

I still ponder these statements today. What I do seems simple to me; so simple that, unfortunately, many who see and experience this process still don't believe it.

THE CASE OF THE GIRL FROM HAWAII

I received a call from Hawaii in May of 1987, asking if I could help a young lady who was possessed by an evil spirit. It seemed better to remove the girl from her environment and bring her to California rather than my going to Hawaii.

Upon their arrival, her mother gave me a tape recording of the facts leading up to and during the girl's problem. From 1956, to 1980, the girl's mother had experienced repeated visits by an incubus, an evil spirit who has sexual intercourse with women while they sleep. Her husband and oldest son, who waited in another room while these attacks were happening, verified these incidents. The attacks stopped after she and her husband became ministers and started doing the Lord's work. During the period of these attacks, she gave birth to three children. The first born of these three was the girl who was brought to see me.

The girl's problem started in 1985, while she was entertaining at a local hotel as a professional dancer. One night, between shows, she walked to the beach to relax. While sitting on the sand a strange man came up behind her and fondled her hair, remarking on how beautiful it was. They talked for a while and when the man departed she had a headache and headaches had been constant since that time.

It was common for her to awake from her sleep feeling that someone was in her bedroom. On April 7, 1987, she experienced an incident of screaming and tearing at her hair. She would laugh, then cry, and then get angry. She became a different personality. On April 13, she had another attack, this time feeling cold. During this assault she spoke fluent Samoan as a male who said he was going to take her with him into the mountains. Following this incident she began eating excessively.

From April to May, 1987, she was seen ten times by five different Kahunas, without success. One attack occurred in church where It took her older brother and several men to restrain her. The stress of these attacks worsened. She had stomach pains that felt "like being screwed from the inside". There was soreness in her breasts and hardness in the vaginal area. Her migraines got worse and she began displaying strange movements in her sleep. She often dreamed that a native chieftain would come and take her to his people in the mountains where women would bow down to her in respect because she was his daughter. A medical CATSCAN had found no physical problem for her expressions.

On May 24, 1987, in the presence of her family an hypnotic evaluation was conducted. She responded well to hypnosis. After induction, she was directed to recall the origin and cause of her problem. During a forty-minute session the following information was obtained.

There was a time in the Polynesian Islands when human sacrifices took place and babies were given to a chieftain for his consumption. In a past life the girl had been offered as a sacrifice by her grandmother . However, when the time came for the sacrifice to take place the grandmother refused to give up the baby. It appeared this chieftain was now demanding his dues. The grandmother, now in spirit, was encouraging the girl to let this chieftain take her. While in hypnosis the girl experienced the presence of this chieftain asking her to go with him. I requested he leave the girl alone and he refused. I then evoked the power of Christ and the entity departed, calling to the girl to come and be with him. After the session she said the instant the chieftain departed she felt as if released from his control.

That night, following the session, the girl dreamed she was sleeping on floor mats between her parents. In her dream the chieftain and five females insisted she go into the mountains with them. She dreamed of crying out to her parents for help and they would not respond. She awoke frightened believing this was another attack. The family called and wanted to bring her back for another session. During the second session she interpreted her dream to simply mean she no longer needed to ask her parents for their help. Contact was then made with the grandmother, in spirit, and I explained our different time and customs. Understanding this, the grandmother then assisted the girl in resisting the demands of the chieftain.

This process apparently worked for, after two days, the family agreed the girl was now displaying her old personality as a beautiful, happy person. I had no further contact with the girl or her family. However, two years later they referred another person from Hawaii to me.

THE CASE OF HELEN

My most interesting experience of working with a subject who was possessed by a negative spirit occurred in the Parks Research and Education Project in 1980. My subject was a woman who had been a victim of incest from the age of four. At age fifteen she gave birth to her father's child. Her mother, and other family members, blamed her for this situation and banished her from their home. She married a man of her own age but proceeded to have sexual affairs with older men. She had absolutely no self-esteem and came to the research project for help to improve this condition.

She responded to the hypnotic induction instantly, entering a somnambulistic state of consciousness. My approach to her problem was to inquire about the first time she experienced the loss of her self-esteem. Immediately following my question she went into a kind of seizure having contortions of her face and shaking of her entire body. She cried out, "He has me and he won't let me go". I said, "Whoever you are, release this woman and leave her alone". The response was, "You don't know who you are talking to". I responded by saying, "And you don't know who you are talking to, so get out and leave her alone". She immediately relaxed and said "He's gone".

I made another appointment with her for a week later. On her return she reported being very tired the entire week and that she had an awful stench about her. I recognized this condition as a sign of spirit possession. This proved to be true. Immediately on entering the hypnotic state, a voice said, "Oh, you're back". I said, "Yes, and I told you to get out and leave this woman alone". At that instant she started having convulsions and crying out that she was being hurt.

A voice in my head said, "You dummy, the Bible tells you how to handle these kinds of problems. Demand in the name of Jesus Christ for the evil spirit to leave the victim's body". I did this and my subject was immediately calm and peaceful. I then asked for a spirit entity from the light to come and be with us. My subject then experienced the presence of a female entity whom I asked what else we could do to help my subject. I was told, "Nothing, now it's up to her". We had a five-year follow-up to this case. Her written response indicated she had no further problems of this nature and she was now living a happy life.

THE CASE OF DAMON

On Monday July 27, 1998, I watched the program 20/20, with Barbara Walters, about Tourette's Syndrome which reminded me of one of my cases back in 1986.

On November 20, 1986, a Mrs. Jones brought her nine-year-old son for me to evaluate his problem with Tourette's. He had had this problem since birth. He was taking two different medications to help control the "Ticks" and other expressions, such as cursing for no apparent reason.

The boy responded well to hypnosis and, during evaluation to determine the origin and cause of this condition, I had him identify the location in his physical system where the problem originated. He mentally observed the upper front area of his brain where he found a "bunch of wires", one of which was broken and black in color. I asked him if he could repair this broken wire and he said yes and stated he would replace it with a gold wire. After he mentally replaced the broken wire I suggested he would experience a tingling sensation starting at the base of his spine, moving up and through the new wire. He related that the tingling started in his toes and circulated through the new wire and back to his toes several times. I then ended the session.

On November 24, 1986, Mrs. Jones phoned to say her son had not needed any medication since the session. She had taken him to a neurologist at the Loma Linda Medical Center, who, after performing a series of tests, stated her son was 90% cured of Tourette's Syndrome.

On December 4, 1986, Mrs. Jones called to say that her son was again having "ticks". She thought it was because his father kept teasing him about his experience with hypnosis. The boy said it was because he wanted the kids at school to tease him as they had done before undergoing hypnosis.

TWO BROTHERS WITH ASTHMA

Two brothers, ages seven and nine, both with a problem of asthma, were brought to me to see if hypnotism could help resolve their problem. I worked individually with them, the younger boy first and the cause of his problem was found to connect to a lack of attention. His family had lived in Florida and a grandmother had taken care of the boys while the parents worked. It then became necessary for the family to move to California. The grandmother came with them but, later, returned to Florida. Shortly afterwards the younger boy started having asthma attacks. These started because he missed the attention his grandmother had given him in the absence of his parents.

When I worked with the older boy I found he started having asthma attacks after seeing, and wanting, the added attention being given to his brother. Both boys learned they could turn these asthma attacks on and off at will. When the parents learned of the boy's control of this expression they no longer responded to their negative actions and, subsequently, the boys stopped having asthma attacks.

Most asthma is the result of feeling the lack of attention or affection. However, asthma can also be associated with too much affection or a feeling of being smothered. As in all cases, a change of emotion must take place to resolve the condition.

THE CASE OF JOHN

When the Parapsychology Association of Riverside, California, held a conference, which was open to the public, a question was asked concerning reincarnation. Some in attendance believed, some disbelieved, and some were on the fence, not sure about this idea. John was one of those on the fence. I told him that if he would attend one of my classes I would help him make up his mind one way or the other. When John attended a class, I hypnotized him and directed him to regress to a time prior to his birth. A facial expression indicated he was having a confused awareness. I asked what he was experiencing, and he replied, "I'm talking with someone, but were not speaking; it's thoughts, like telepathy." I asked him what year it was and he replied "4000 BC". I then asked if he believed in God and he said, "God is the system". When I asked what he meant, he said, "I mean it's better to be in the system than out of it". When I asked why we don't, or can't, use this system now, he said, "Because you are in a new beginning. You will be doing it in your year 3000".

Regressions with other people have indicated we are in a third beginning, which is getting close to ending. When we take people into the future, between the years 2600 and 3000, telepathy is their manner of communication.

One lady who was taken ahead to this time period said she was born to communicate telepathically. She was a "Monitor", keeping track of space vehicles moving throughout the universe. She lived in a domed city in the sky which was limited in population and self sufficient as to the needs of the population. When asked if she knew about Earth she said, "No, I'm not programmed for that". She had been programmed by a machine and was not aware of the terms "United States" or "Earth". When she was not working she used a space scooter to go to a rest area, much like a park. She was in this rest area during our communication. While we were talking her elbow moved as though pushing someone away. When I questioned this movement she said a male friend wanted her to stop talking with me and to pay more attention to him.

THE CASE OF THE SHEEPHERDER

It is a fact that in hypnotism the further away from conscious awareness one goes the less awareness there is of time. In the deep subconscious time doesn't exist. The past, present and future are one. If this is true it should be possible to change the past experience of an individual by the process of hypnotic regression.

Several years ago I did a past life regression with a man whose profession was electrical engineering and he was a very knowledgeable and educated individual. During a regression to a past life he identified himself as a fifty-two-year-old sheepherder somewhere in Spain. After answering a few questions he said "Mister, I'm a simple man. I don't know what you are talking about. If you want to talk about sheep or dogs I'll talk to you".

I then regressed him to the age of twenty and found him to be a tanner in a leather factory making leather aprons. He gave his name as Greeg and he had a friend named Gooso. For recreation they would go to a tavern and have a beer. Gooso, a mason, would talk about bricks and he would talk about leather.

I suggested he take me to the tavern to meet Gooso and we could all have a beer. His next response was, "Hey, Gooso, I have this thing that talks to me. Let's buy him a beer and I'll drink it". I said, "How about me? I wouldn't mind having a beer". Greeg responded with, "Mister, just who in the hell are you? I hear you, but I can't see you".

Getting the impression Greeg was talking to himself I asked him what they did about people in his town who talked to themselves. He replied, "They send them out to herd sheep!" Was it my contact with Greeg that caused him to become a sheepherder later in his life?

I asked if there was anyone in his community who was of any notability. He said, "There's Jakes who can read and write, and there's a guy up north named Napoleon who is trying to make a name for himself but he will burn himself out, they all do."

THE CASE OF SANDY

Sometimes there's a feeling, a knowing, that a person can be relieved of his affliction. So it was in the case of a man with a drooping eyelid. When we first met his left eyelid completely covered his eye while the right eye was wide open. He lifted the lid with his fingers, showing he could see from the eye but could not control the lid. He gave me the medical term for the problem and said there was no cure for the condition. The doctors had told him the nerves in his forehead, which controlled the eyelid, were dead and that eventually the right eyelid would fail, and then his entire face. I told him the cause behind his condition and suggested he attend my convention workshop that day, assuring him that I would help resolve his problem. There was no doubt in my mind that I could help him recover the system. He told me that several other hypnotists had tried without success. I wondered if he would give it one more try.

He came to my workshop and allowed me to use him to demonstrate my process to the rest of the class. It took just fourteen minutes to take him through the reconstruction of the past negative emotional experiences, which were behind his problem. When he awakened from the hypnotic attitude both eyes opened and have remained normal for more than two years now. Following the session he admitted I had been right as to the cause of the problem. He had not liked seeing the offensive actions of a female friend. By resolving the emotions of these past experiences he also resolved the physical condition.

THE CASE OF LAURA

While visiting with friends in Vancouver, Washington, I was asked if hypnotherapy could help a young girl of eight. On several occasions recently, after everyone had gone to bed, the daughter, crying hysterically, would awaken her parents. They would find her standing in the middle of the living room with her eyes shut as if still asleep. The parents told us it had been difficult to wake her and, when they did, she would not remember how she had got out of bed and into the living room.

I went to the parent's home to visit with the girl. She was a shy young lady and seemed uncomfortable around strangers. I suggested I work with Laura, the mother, and try to make a connection. The following day Laura was hypnotized and asked to make connection with her daughter's dreams. After the session Laura seemed to feel she had a better understanding of it. This seemed to work and, in a few days, I left town. Almost two years later I had occasion to visit with the family and was again in the presence of the young daughter, now age ten. When Laura asked the girl if she remembered me her comment was, "Yes, he is the man who worked with me and made my bad dreams stop". Of course, this was a surprise to all of us. Laura tried to convince her daughter that I had not worked with her but it was to no avail.

Recently I visited with this charming young lady who still insists that I worked with her. Who I worked with, or how, is really of no significance, only the final result is important. Whatever the problem was this child has not found it necessary to experience any further bad dreams. The mind truly works in strange and wonderful ways. We simply do not know what we can do until we try.

Chapter Fourteen
"THE STREAM"

(And other topics)

Imagination is what forms our personality. In 1972 I developed a method to identify one's personality by the way they imagined this little story I call "The Stream". Imagination is the creative force behind thought. Thoughts and imagination are our only reality. Are thoughts and imagination hereditary, or is thought a separate independent entity, a part of a unique individual creation? It is recognized that each newborn has the power of thought and a distinct personality. Personality seems to be formed by the way we imagine experiences. The personality of a newborn can be the result of previous experiences.

Each experience is recorded as it is imagined emotionally. Imagination forms our personality. Therefore, future thought is based upon the personality that was formed by imagination. If thought is the foundation of our emotions then thought is also the builder of our personality. Thought is an independent choice of the individual. Therefore, we create our own realities.

The way we imagine an experience is a representation of our personality. For example, "Imagine you are taking a walk in the country and you come upon a stream flowing across in front of you. At this point determine the width of the stream from one bank to the other, how deep the water is, the speed and texture of the water. The width of the stream is the number of feet from one bank to the other. Measure the depth by walking through the water and determining how high on your body the water comes at its constant level. The texture of the water is crystal clear, murky or dirty. Count any rocks sticking out of the water and determine if they are smooth or sharp."

The way you observe this stream defines your personality. The width, depth, speed and texture of the water each represent apart of your personality. You may imagine a stream that is familiar. It may be where you have fished or vacationed, or from movies and pictures you have seen. It doesn't make any difference. The mind selects from all the streams you have seen and chooses the one which represents your personality.

Imagination is very real when it comes to the Reconstruction of past experiences. When the imagination and the willpower are in conflict with each other the imagination will always win.

The Width of the stream (number of feet from one bank to the other) represents the expanse of the individuals associations. One who works with the public would imagine a wider stream than a loner or homebody. The average width is from three to six feet.

The Depth of the water represents the depth of these associations. The deeper the water the more the individual is involved emotionally with these associations. The average depth when walking through the water is from the calf to the knee.

The Speed of the water represents the way life is being experienced. Slow indicates inactivity. Medium indicates normal activity. Fast indicates an active or busy life. A person who is very busy and imagines the water is moving medium or slow likes their work or activity and it is easy for them. The person who is inactive and imagines the water moving fast is emotionally stressed and needs help.

The Texture of the water represents an overall self-opinion including moral values and physical condition. Murky or dirty water indicates there is something going on in the life of the individual that needs to be cleared or cleaned up.

Rocks are Problems. Rocks, bushes and changes in the flow of the stream all have a meaning representing the personality. Rocks on the bottom of the stream are not interfering with life. Rocks showing above the water are problems currently affecting the flow of life. Smooth rocks suggest the problems have been there a long time. Sharp rocks indicate the problems are new. When emotion has been directed toward a male the rocks are on the side closest to you. Rocks on the opposite side of the stream indicate the emotion has been directed toward a female. Rocks in the middle of the stream represent a situation or condition rather than emotions being directed at a male or female. A change in the direction of the stream indicates a change in life. A fork would represent a decision to be made. Up stream represents the past, down stream the future.

Your stream will represent the way you imagine your life to be. Change your imagination and you will change your life.

During the Parks Research & Education Project one of the volunteers came to evaluate his problem with schizophrenia. A few years earlier he was a dental technician on a military ship. An incident on the ship had caused the death of two of his shipmates. As he and his friends were discussing the responsibility of the government for these deaths he became so emotional that he begin hallucinating. He was eventually discharged and sent to a veteran's hospital where they treated his illness with drugs. This drug would last about a month at a time. When he started hallucinating again he would return to the hospital for another treatment.

While during the initial interview at the PREP he started hallucinating faces of people and hearing voices in his head. At this point I asked him to imagine my stream. On doing this he said, "But I see two different streams and they are running parallel to each other". I took this to mean that one stream represented the conscious mind and the other the subconscious mind. I suggested he merge these two streams and make them one. On doing this the images and voices in his head stopped. My understanding of his problem was that the incident on the ship opened the door between the conscious and subconscious mind and the door was never shut. The merging of the two streams in imagination closed this door.

THE CONTROVERSY OVER THE CAUSE OF HOMOSEXUALITY

Both as a police officer and hypnotherapist I have counseled many men and women who were living a homosexual lifestyle. Looking into the cause of this way of life, I have inquired if this condition was present at birth or if it is learned. In every case I found the cause to be the lack of bonding with the parent of the same gender, men with their fathers, girls with their mothers. I believe this expression can be changed but few choose to consider this lack of bonding to be the cause of homosexuality. Some who have tried to reconcile with their parent found them resistant in considering responsibility. There may also be a past life connection to this expression. Of course not all of those lacking bonding become homosexual.

There seems to be more homosexuality now than was apparent in the past. Are people simply more willing to reveal this lifestyle today? Could this be a result in the trend toward single and unmarried parents and the break down of the family unit? I continue to look for patterns to answer this question.

COMA

A local attorney referred a teen-aged boy who had been involved in an auto accident in which two other people had been killed. The boy was found unconscious at the scene of the accident and taken to a hospital where he remained in a coma for a week. After he awakened from this condition he could not remember anything from a week before the accident to a week after.

He responded well to hypnosis and, during a thirty-minute session, I learned he had borrowed the car from a girlfriend and had then picked up two male friends to go riding. One friend insisted on driving the car so he got in the back seat as a passenger. His friend ran a stop sign and hit another car killing the two occupants. His car was knocked into a telephone pole and split in half and he remembered flying out of the back seat and hitting the ground. He saw his two buddies get out of the car and run from the scene. His next awareness was of someone beating on his chest and then taking him to the hospital. Under hypnosis he remembered his family coming to visit and not being able to talk or move. When I asked how he felt about the situation he replied that he felt his parents could have been more concerned about his condition than they were.

Because he was the only one the police found alive at the scene of the accident he was thought to be the driver of one of the cars. He had been charged with causing the accident and the death of two people. The information obtained through hypnosis was given to the police to assist them in their investigation. The final outcome of this case is unknown to me.

It is not uncommon to experience a loss of conscious memory after being in a coma. However, there is no loss of memory in the subconscious. Hypnosis has been a successful method of bringing this information to conscious awareness and we have learned from coma patients that they can be fully aware of what is going on around them but are simply unable to bring this awareness to a conscious level.

UNCONSCIOUS AWARENESS

A businessman who was going to speak to a large group of people was doubtful of his ability to do this and hypnotism was suggested as a way for him to prepare. I went to his home, hypnotized him as he lay on the floor in the living room, and the session lasted approximately ten minutes. During this time I assured him that he had the ability to do public speaking. When we finished he got up to pay me and went directly to a bedroom and removed some money from a dresser drawer at which time his wife, looking and acting surprised, asked him how he knew the money was there as, upon arriving home that night, they had put the money in a kitchen cabinet. While her husband was hypnotized she had taken the money from the kitchen cabinet and put it in a bedroom dresser drawer. Neither understood how he knew the money had been moved.

Was he consciously aware of the sounds his wife made while moving the money? Or, is there really more to our subconscious awareness then we presently have knowledge of?

LOST AND FOUND

Memory can often be enhanced with hypnotism and there are times when a hypnotic induction is not obvious to the subject. I was called to the home of an elderly lady who could not find an expensive diamond ring. We sat down at her dining room table to talk about hypnotism and, almost immediately, before I even started talking about the induction process, she appeared to be tired and sleepy. I suggested she take a nap and when she awakened she would know where she had placed her ring. She went to her bed to nap and I prepared to leave. I told her son that, when she awakened, if she was able to locate her ring he could send me a check. If the ring were not found there would be no charge. A short time after I returned home her son called to say the check was in the mail as immediately on awakening, his mother had gone to a dresser drawer and located her ring wrapped in a handkerchief.

WHEN WE BELIEVE WHAT WE HEAR

After I retired from police service I took a job teaching an Administration of Justice course at a local community college. Only one student, who scored but 56 out of 100, failed the first examination I gave. His records indicated he had a learning disability and was being tutored in a special class at the college. I talked to him about trying hypnosis to find out why he had this problem. In one session I learned that his parents used to tell him and his brother, "You know you're retarded, why don't you act like it"? We worked out the emotional connection to this statement and he was assured he could do better. On the next examination he scored a 98 out of 100. He went on to pass my class with an over-all grade of "A".

This is a good example of words and actions being repeated often enough to become accepted in the subconscious. As with an affirmation, the words accepted become your reality. We find the loss of self-esteem is caused by acceptance of the words or actions of someone else, someone who is simply voicing their own personal opinion. And personal opinions can be wrong. No longer should anyone allow the words and actions of others to offend our self-esteem.

In all my experience I have never found a person who has not lost his/her self-esteem at some time during life. This is one of the first evaluations I make during a therapy session. I never cease to be surprised how "simple words" can cause intense negative emotions that are always with us until resolved at the point where they were imprinted in the subconscious.

INCEST

In my work I have found Incest to be the most damaging emotion one can experience. This damage is not caused until the victim determines it to be wrong. Most of my cases of incest started when the victim was four to five years old. In one case however, the abuse started when the girl was eleven years of age. Her father molested her a total of six times, then stopped. When I inquired as to the cause or reason for this my subject regressed to a past life. She said, "I am in a position of power and authority; I have offended this man. This man is now my father. This was his first opportunity to teach me a lesson in the misuse of power and authority". Karma is an important part of this experience and will be discussed more in Chapter fourteen.

TELEKINESIS

Telekinesis is the production of motion in objects (as by a spiritualistic medium) without contact or other physical means.

A spirit entity was asked, during a regression, if it was possible for us to move an object with our mind. His response was "Yes. This is possible when the vision of the eyes and the vision of the mind corresponds. You concentrate on an object until it appears as a bright light. Then synchronize your mind with the object and the thought of what you want to do. This causes the force to move the object. This should be done with the eyes open. A way to practice this is by placing a toothpick in a pan of water and mentally moving it across the water. Another method is to look at an apple and feel you are the apple. Identify yourself with that which makes the apple".

EGYPTIAN REGRESSION

One of my subjects regressed to a life as a farmer in ancient Egypt and I asked him about the building of the pyramids. He said they were built as a thing of beauty and a monument to the Pharaoh's. They were constructed by using ropes, pulleys and certain men gifted in the art of levitation.

I found this interesting because I have watched several television programs which stated that they (present day builders) have not been able to duplicate the building of the pyramids by using ropes, pulleys and ramps alone.

VORTEX

A vortex is described as a mass of fluid (as a liquid) with a whirling or circular motion, which tends to form a cavity or vacuum in the center of the circle and to draw toward this cavity, or vacuum, bodies subject to its action.

In order to make space travel more plausible, scientists are trying to find a speed greater than light, which is essential if we are to accomplish this feat in one generation.

In 1972, during a regression, I was told that, on earth, there are several locations where vortexes can make this feat possible one of which is located in what we know as the Bermuda Triangle. Once in a vortex one can be transported through space without a protective shield, and without harm, at a rate of motion greater than the speed of light. Thought, of course, is the greatest speed possible.

Hibernation is another method we will use to cope with time as has been done by other species. I believe we will develop this process before we attempt to enter a vortex.

WORDS FROM ANOTHER DIMENSION

Others in the spiritual realm tell me there are other forms and units of energies that exist. Some planets are in the process of growing and developing while others are dying out. The principles which pertain to planets are the same principles that pertain to, and affect, us.

Denotica (refer to chapter twelve) said she believed there are presently ten planets in our solar system, one yet to be discovered further out. Astronomers have believed there is another planet outside of Pluto but it hasn't been discovered yet. There is a body near the sun, which is very small and we don't, or won't, know if it should be called a moon or a planet. Denotica also said our galaxy has two major systems; Good and evil. Evil is against kindness. There are two suction systems, known as Black Holes. One picks up debris, and the other is an evil force, a weapon of war.

She mentioned that low voltage static electricity will be used to push apart the molds, or cancer cells, making them harmless. The use of this energy will also be used to treat multiple sclerosis as weak cells in the brain cause this condition. This brain area will be stimulated in the same manner that we restart the heart. Everything must be in its time; any jump ahead can ruin another plan and we will develop these instruments when the time is right.

Denotica also said our earth's magnetic poles are primitive and not in the right area. Our instruments do not give the correct, or true, magnetic north.

We also have this static electricity within our own bodies and can mentally explore the inner body of an ill person using it to then push out the evil, which is not good and goes against the ten rules. (Refer to chapter 12 the case of Denotica and the healing circle)

Each person has a blueprint in his mind DNA (Deoxyribonucleic Acid). DNA is generally associated with the size, shape, weight, height, and looks of our ancestors. I believe it also contains the plan of our life, which was predetermined before we entered into our present life experience. Some can be changed and some was predetermined not to be changed.

We find many people are willing to live with a diagnosis simply because they have been told it is hereditary and we can allow the word 'hereditary' to become a self-fulfilling prophecy. In regression we often find it was the individual's choice to be born into a particular family for a specific experience necessary for growth. Hypnosis can sometimes help change this blueprint.

TIME AND SPACE

We are in the general notion of the speed of light and sound. There are some who can eliminate this concept and hence, by thought, are able to eliminate space and time.

Almost every person in a hypnotic regression, when speaking of time, says there is no such thing in the spiritual realm. They know it as we do when relating to the material world but, in the spiritual realm, time does not apply. Even in the simple process of hypnosis many subjects are amazed at their unawareness of the passage of time. The apparent action of material thought at any given moment is merely due to our limited senses, which prevent us from being conscious of any thought either before or after it comes into action. When you recognize that the material world has nothing to do with your real self you will see there is no such thing as time. What we perceive of the universe is only the impression produced by our senses. The form we give to things is conditioned by the nature of our intelligence. Time and space then are subjective notions imposed by our senses on the representation of things. Time is, for man, nothing but a relation between events.

As Kant pointed out, "Space and Time do not concern things as they are in themselves but only as they appear to our senses, being limitations imposed on the human mind by its very nature".

REINCARNATION

In the preceding pages, the reader has found reference to reincarnation, re-cycle of the soul, vibrations, auras, etc., the meaning of which are often times misinterpreted. Take reincarnation for example. This term is often confused with transmigration, being re-born in another life form such as plant or animal. Reincarnation indicates a separation of the soul and body at death, and are only a change of the vibrational force to another dimension of thought.

During a regression I asked, "If we come from God and are trying to get back to God, what happens when we get there?" The immediate answer was "You cease to be, and yet you are, as you become that which you have always been".

Considering the information given by people in hypnotic regression I compare their interpretations with some of the world's greatest thinkers. Many were in favor of the theory of reincarnation.

Kant wrote, "If we should see the things and ourselves as they are we should see ourselves in a world of spiritual natures with which our entire real relation neither began at birth nor ended with the body's death".

Sir Edwin Arnold wrote, "Never the spirit is born, the spirit will cease to be never, never was a time it was not, end and beginning are dreams".

Richard Jefferies wrote, "Now is eternity, now I am in the midst of immortality".

Longfellow wrote, "There is no death! What seems so is transition".

Doctor LeBon said, "Nature knows no rest; the whole of what is called a dead body is a mass of so-called life, molecules vibrating with terrific rapidity".

"That which hath been is now, and that which is to be hath already been, and God requireth that which is past". (Ecclesiastics 3:15).

F.L. Rawson, in his book, Life Understood, claims that reality is only God and His mental or spiritual manifestations and that matter and evil are unreal. Mathematically we know that anything that ever was, was nothing, or ever ceases to exist, or cannot be real. Nothing evil or imperfect can possibly last, as it is self-destructive. The so-called material world is only a world of constantly shifting appearances, false illusions, so-called phenomena and every form of matter, every form of sin, every form of disease and trouble can be caused to appear and disappear by what is falsely termed "thinking". This is because all matter is ethereal (of the ether), the ether consisting of lines of forces at right angles to each other Which are usually spoken of as thoughts. Therefore, thoughts are things.

Annie Wood Besant (1847-1933), Founder of the Central Hindu College at Banaras, India, wrote, "The proofs of reincarnation do not amount to a complete and general demonstration but they establish as strong a presumption as can, in the nature of the case, exist. The theory they support affords the only sufficient explanation of the growth and decay of nations, of the facts in individual evolution, of the varying capacities of man, of recurrent cycles in history, of unique human characters. I am content, despite my own certain knowledge, that reincarnation is a fact in nature".

To those who have not found satisfaction in the material world, I refer you to these words of Dr. Albert Schweitzer: "The only ones among you who will be really happy are those who have sought and found how to serve." There are some who search for larger truths and, in the quest, sense the joy of immortality

Ha-ha-ha! laughed Pierre. And he said aloud to himself, "The soldier did not let me pass. They took me and shut me up. They held me captive. What me? My immortal soul? Ha-ha-ha! Ha-ha-ha!," and he laughed till tears started to his eyes. A man got up and came to see what this queer big fellow was laughing at all by himself. Pierre stopped laughing, got up, went further away from the inquisitive man, and looked around him. The huge, endless bivouac that had previously resounded with the crackling of campfires and the voices of many men had grown quiet, the red campfires were growing paler and dying down. High up in the light sky hung the full moon. Forests and fields beyond the camp, unseen before, were now visible in the distance. And farther still, beyond those forests and fields, the bright, oscillating, limitless distance lured one to itself. Pierre glanced up at the sky and twinkling stars in its faraway depths. And all that is me, all that is within me, and it is all I, thought Pierre. And they caught all that and put it into a shed boarded up with planks! He smiled, and went and laid down to sleep beside his companions (Tolstoy, War and Peace)

Chapter Fifteen
THE MYSTERY OF SPIRIT ATTACHMENT

And Other Responses in Hypnotherapy

Every hypnotists, who has spent time doing hypnotic regressions, has experienced the phenomena of spirit attachment, or spirit possession, to their subjects. Some of these therapists choose to avoid or ignore these expressions while others make it their sole purpose to work with and understand this mystery. I choose to work with them as they occur. This phenomena happens much more frequent than one may imagine. I am sure that some of the other therapy professions look at this as an emotional disorder rather than to consider its reality. The following are some of my experiences with spirit attachments and other responses during the process of hypnotherapy.

During the course of my experiences in hypnotic age regression I learned of spirit attachments to present life individuals. As these spirits come from different spiritual levels some are of a negative influence. I was taught these spirits could be challenged to see if they came from God or not. To the challenge, "Do you come from the light?" a simple yes comes from those who are of the light, or God. An entity not from the light cannot lie and their response is a diversion like, "I see the light, or, the light is above me, or a simple no".

During a regression session in one of my classes my female subject suddenly stated, "I'm talking with Christ". Someone in the class called out, "Challenge that entity". I said to the entity, "Do you come from the light?" In a strong commanding voice the response was, "I AM THE LIGHT". The young lady experiencing this incident enquired on becoming a nun. After a short service in the Francisco Order she returned home and has since developed the expression of a psychic medium.

In other sections of this book spiritual levels are mentioned and described. It appears that each of us is at a level of spiritual knowledge about our lives. As we learn to live the truths of our creation we move up to higher spiritual levels. Those up to level six are the takers, persons who take from others without giving anything in return. Then between levels six & seven there is an emotion of conflict, wanting to give but wanting help in doing it. The higher we go the more we can give to others. The saying

"Give till it hurts," means one has reached their maximum level and should not attempt to give more if it hurts to do it. I have found that those who say they don't believe in reincarnation are always at level three or below.

One of my clients wanted me to help him break away from a relationship with a woman. Even though they had separated, and he had no further contact with her he could not get her off his mind.

During the session a spirit entity made its presence known. The attitude of this spirit attachment was not of a positive nature so I asked what level he was coming from. His response was, "Minus nine asshole". Taken somewhat off-guard with this response I tried to carry on a conversation as to his connection with my client. When he refused to communicate with me I evoked the power of Christ to separate him from this connection. When I awakened my client his first statement was, "what was that, some kind of exorcism"? He then said that the moment this spirit entity departed the feeling he had for this woman also left him.

In 1963 I was told that human cloning would occur in my lifetime. The likeness will be there but without a SOUL. I was also told that the moment of conception involves the greatest force in the universe. I have regressed at least two persons through the moment of conception. At that instant their bodies moved as if jolted by some instant force.

Several incidents where a person was born in the breach position suggested they were trying to back out of their commitment to the birth experience. Rejection at birth is also a common occurrence. During a hypnotic regression with a middle-aged man he was directed to recall his first experience of feeling rejected. He regressed to his birth experience and stated, "They threw me in a trash can". When he was born the doctor thought he was dead and tossed him in a trashcan. A nurse checked and found him alive.

A lady near the age of sixty had felt rejected all of her life. In hypnotism she was directed to recall the first time she experienced the feeling of rejection. She also went to her birth experience and found she was born a twin. Being the first-born they had placed her across the room on a shelf and returned to deliver her brother. Being placed alone on this shelf she felt she was being rejected. Following this hypnotic experience she no longer felt this negative emotion.

A 26 year old lady came to me so stressed she cried most of the interview. She resisted the induction process until further informed about hypnosis. She told me that as a child going to the Catholic Church, a nun told her she could breathe in the devil. Whenever she yawns or breathes heavy she thinks she is taking in the devil. She feels unclean even though she is doing nothing bad or evil. She was worried about being possessed by an evil spirit and was being negative about everything.

During a twenty-minute session she was directed to experience the awareness of a spirit entity from the light. From this entity she learned she was at spiritual level eleven. She was directed to replace her negative emotions to positive expressions. When she left my office she was all smiles, feeling good, and I think understanding how to overcome her negative emotions.

On December 30, 1986 Mike came to me with the desire to stop smoking. He was a big man with an almost perfect body. I wondered why a person of his stature would be a smoker. He informed me he was a bodybuilder and this was his first experience with hypnosis. At first there was some resistance to the induction process. However, during a twenty-minute session he experienced the following.

He had his first cigarette at the age of thirteen. He became addicted one year later. He started smoking to impress himself & others. He found ten additional experiences where this attitude reinforced the habit. During my process of mentally cleansing the body systems of the contamination of smoking he reacted by shaking, gasping for air and twice thought he was going to vomit. His first thought after the session was to go to his car and destroy the cigarettes he had left there. He was determined he would not smoke again.

One month later he requested another session to work on developing the calves of his legs. He reported he had not smoked since his first visit. During this session he recalled working out with Mr. California, another bodybuilder, in 1981. He was told that he would never be able to build that part of his body, that black men could never build big calves, and he believed it. He was directed through my process of clearing this and other negative experiences connected to building his body. It was suggested that growth of the calves would start immediately and that his body chemicals and energy systems would adjust to increase his potential to develop all body systems. It was also suggested that no one would be able to defeat his efforts by their negative words and actions. Magnetic passes were also made over the knees and legs. It was also suggested that he would experience the sensations of heat and stimulation every time he was involved in the exercise of these systems.

Following the session he said he had experienced the suggested sensations and had been both mentally and physically aware of me passing my hands over these body areas, even though I had not touched him. He has already had improvement in the size and power of his calves. He has become very responsive to hypnotism. I worked with Mike 26 times during a five-year period.

One of my processes to accomplish self-hypnosis is to use the imagination in going down a flight of stairs, opening a door, placing a chair on the other side of the door, putting someone in the chair and communicating about a predetermined purpose. Mike had been shown this process. On March 12, 1987 he asked for another session. He had been practicing self-hypnosis but was afraid to open the door. He knew he would find his deceased brother on the other side of the door. He said that while trying to do self-hypnosis his brother's dog, who is now seventeen years old, was trying to get into his room. He thought that if he made contact with his brother the dog would die.

I helped Mike to make mental contact with his brother in the spirit world. When contact was made with his brother's spirit communication between them continued for the rest of the session. It was learned that it was through the efforts of his brother that he, Mike, had been brought in contact with me. When Mike first saw me he was frightened, not knowing if I represented something good or bad. He said his brother's spirit said he knew me and that he was there to help Mike understand. Mike said that when his brother was living his brother always looked up to him with respect, but he had always treated him like dirt. He has felt guilty since his brother's death, but now it has been resolved.

A week later Mike said he was a much happier person. His lady told him he was more human and looked younger. At this session it was suggested that body builders who have passed on to the spirit world would offer him information about new and better training methods, mental & emotional attitudes, and mind body connections. He was also directed to mentally project to a future event where he had won a championship. To relate to the size, shape, and strength of the body in championship form.

At a session on March 26, 1987 we evaluated headaches that were contributed to his use of steroids in the past. Mike has not used steroids or tobacco since his first session. He was directed to see and feel his body, mind, and spirit merging as one. On doing this he mentally observed an open door at the back of his head, as though seeing through his body. On going through this door he was so elated he threw his arms wide and sighed from pleasure. He described entering the color purple beyond the door. When he returned to his starting point the door closed. He said his health, strength, and emotional attitudes were so much better he couldn't explain the change, but he loves it.

At another session Mike reported that he is no longer being kidded about his shape and strength. Other people in body building are in fact helping him try new methods of training, people who had not volunteered before his last session. He said he has been able to match the conditions, which had required steroids to accomplish before hypnosis. He is very pleased to have made such drastic improvements without drugs.

One day Mike called to report a stomach problem that was causing much pain. It was determined to be coming from the colon area and connected to a relationship with a woman in 1982. The woman terminated the relationship in 1984 against his wishes. It was doing a time of remembering their relationship that the emotion and pain occurred. A spirit entity advised the problem would be relieved in two days.

During another session Mike experienced awareness that he was in the year 1090 Rome Italy as a man named Uleuses, an entertainer, who was pleasing a crowd by lifting large rocks above his head. He said a bodybuilder at best loses only eight pounds a year in preparing for a contest. Since his first visit, ten months ago, he has lost forty pounds yet increased the size and shape of his body.

In October Mike begin having troubles on his job. He had started smoking again, 2 to 3 cigarettes a day for two weeks. In this session he determined he was on his present job to teach his supervisor a lesson in the use of power & authority. He is the only one on the job who stands up to the misuse of authority by his supervisor. He determined that within six months he would be on a job of high security. In May Mike said he was working as a bodyguard and limo driver.

In December of 1988 Mike started having colds and the flu. This problem continued June of 1989. He wanted to explore the reason for this condition. During a thirty-minute session he experienced the following. It was suggested that the spirit of his brother would assist. He said that his brother appeared as a blue light then stepped aside to expose a red light that represented a negative spirit named Jason. Jason said he was Mike's higher positive self. He then exposed Mike's higher negative self who was identified as Julie Ann. Mike was directed to determine when this negative spirit attached to him. He said he was in the Philippines with his father when he was eight years old. He and his father and brother went into a house they were moving into. While there Mike felt the presence of a homicide victim in the bathtub. The spirit of this victim attached to Mike because of his awareness. Julie Ann was described as being 129 years old and evil. Julie Ann identified an evil female who had been in Mike's present life experiences. This spirit refused to talk directly to me so she was directed in the name of Jesus Christ to detach from Mike. When this was done he experienced a relief as if something had been removed from his stomach. The spirit had hidden its face on departing.

Mike said he had been dating a lady for about one and a half years. She died recently and after her death he learned she had been deceiving him, living a lie, and this is what started him smoking again. His smoking connected to the emotions of loss and fear. His boredom, being alone and not caring was the cause. My last visit with Mike was October 29, 1991

This case is an example of how we can be so positive one day and so down and negative the next. It is our choice of thought, negative or positive, in our experiences that determine our well-being. Each negative emotion, if not resolved in a reasonable period of time, will offend the physical system connected to the emotion.

A thirty-three old woman came to me to see if hypnosis would help lose weight. She also said she would like to have children but she has never had a menstrual period. The doctors have diagnosed her problem as Polycystic Ovary Syndrome.

During a seventeen-minute session she experienced an awareness that her weight problem first started when she was eight years old. The problem was related to the emotions of the fear of being abandoned. We found a past life experience in 1763 where as a seventeen year old girl she had abandoned a child. Following the session she remarked that she has always had a problem with children and had determined she did not want to bear any. At age three in her present life she experienced the emotion of abandonment for the first time. At the age of eleven she started to have her first menstrual period but it stopped after a few spots. At that time she was again experiencing the feeling of abandonment.

She determined she will lose 120 pounds of weight in the next ten months, and she will start having her menstrual period within the next six months. The date of this session was April 21st, 2001.

On February 13, 1987 Michael came to me to evaluate an attitude about his fear of succeeding. During the next four years we had sixteen more sessions finding and resolving connections to this problem. The first connection we found was when he was three years old in his present life. He had accomplished or done something he was proud of but for some unknown reason his mother had responded by hitting him in the stomach several times. He connected this experience to the emotion of disappointment. He also recalled that his father had a habit of hitting him in the stomach up to the age of sixteen when he left home. During this session I observed a twitching and shaking of his stomach.

At a session in 1989 Michael was asked if he had a spirit attachment with him. He said that at the age of five he was riding in a pickup truck with his grandfather. As he was enjoying the scenery of the country they passed a farmhouse where a boy named Jerry just died and his spirit attached to him. Jerry was a poor farm boy who had the deformity of being unable to speak (Autistic) and wanted to be taken care of so as to be able to achieve something that he could not do on his own. Jerry was present during this session and did not want to separate from Michael even though he knew he had to leave. By the power of Jesus Christ he was directed to separate from Michael and continue his journey to the light. Michael went through hundreds of previous experiences where Jerry had influenced him in a negative manner. During this session he twisted & shook, and his mouth distorted while Jerry was being encouraged to leave. Following the session he said the session was more successful than all the rest put together.

The next session revealed that when he was just one day old he was aware that his mother did not love him. At the ages of five, seven, and fifteen, he wanted recognition for something he had accomplished but was shunned by both his mother and father, therefore adding to the emotion of "fear of succeeding". When directed to recall a time in the past when he was a success and had leadership and authority abilities he experienced awareness of a past life where he had been the owner and operator of a shipping business. He had three ships handling freight and passengers to East India.

Directing him to see if there was any past life connection to his "fearing to succeed" he told of being a six-year old living in Ohio and being made to use a horse and plow to do the fields. Being able to do this he was made to do most of his fathers work so his father could roam. Eventually they moved from Ohio to Missouri where his father became a trapper. He grew to resent the responsibility of doing his fathers work. One day at his age of sixteen, while he and his father were away from home, Indians burned their cabin and killed his mother and sister. His father blamed him for their deaths so he left home and headed for California. At the age of twenty-two, in the Kansas Territory, he was shot by an Indian and then nursed back to health by an Indian squaw. At the age of twenty-six he was killed by an Indian in Colorado.

Another session was held to confront an issue involving his relationships with women. At the time of these sessions Michael was seeing three different women simultaneously. I hypnotized and regressed two of them. One had been a student in my hypnosis classes and it was she who referred Michael to me. This woman had shown some resistance to hypnosis due to the fear of the unknown, and she didn't believe in reincarnation. She had wanted to evaluate her low self-esteem. I worked with her six times before she felt safe enough to allow responses to my directions. During one of my classes a woman who did psychic channeling told her she saw her in a past life as an Indian maiden who loved a man that was with her in her present life.

On April 25 1987 she regressed to a past life where she was getting water from a stream. She gave her name as Char; she had long black hair in two braids, she was fourteen years old. She said she had been lost from her tribe and a white man with a tall hat (Stovepipe type) found her and traded her to another Cheyenne tribe. She had been given to an old woman of the tribe. Her duties were to carry water and pound grain.

When she was eighteen years old she was at a stream getting water when she saw a white man fall from his horse, he was sick and bleeding from a wound in the left side of his body. She found a piece of wood in the wound. She hid him in the woods and took care of him for several months, bringing him food and medicine from her camp. If the braves had found him they would have killed him. She said the man had warm eyes like an animal, his name was Ben and he was twenty-two years old. She grew to love him because his eyes were warm and sensitive, but he had to leave before the braves found him. After he left she returned to camp and found the braves had killed the old lady for not telling the truth about where she was. They beat her and she spent the rest of her life doing chores. She aged rapidly because of too many chores and died at the age of forty-seven. Moving into the spiritual realm following her death she found the man she had helped was also there but he didn't recognize her. He entered another life and she chose to follow him, "as she loved the one beyond the eyes". She also learned from this session that the man who found her and traded her to the Cheyenne tribe is her father in her present life. In the past he had been an evil man and was with her now to have the attachment to learn, and that he had learned.

Another woman in Michael's life came to see me about being overweight and frightened of being alone. In a third session she regressed to a past life experience where she was walking hand in hand with a young man beside a wagon train heading west from the Kansas Territory. One day this young man road off and never returned. This young man is now with her as Michael. In a previous regression Michael had spoken of an experience where he was walking hand in hand with a woman beside a wagon train. When he left her he had no intention of returning to her. In their present relationship a negative emotion is not yet resolved.

When Michael was in high school a teacher told him he would succeed greatly if he would only leave the women alone. He has had five involved relationships, two ended in marriage. None of these relationships lasted more than 3 1/2 years. It was found that all of these five associations involved the emotions of forgiveness, compassion, trust, security, and fear. The origin of these motions started from his birth experience of being rejected by his mother. He had the same feeling toward his father at the age of six months. From this birth experience stems the pattern of his unstable relationships. As a child he felt he was just taking to anyone who wanted him, staying until he was put down, and someone else picked him up. These women put him down because he would not commit himself to the emotion of love. The emotion of forgiveness related to the death of his mother in the past life. Compassion related to the nurse at his birth in his present life. Security related to the life as a ship owner. Fear related to his sister of the past life, fear of not forgiving him for her death and not being present when it happened. He has had a very hard time relating to the emotion of love. He determined the reason he cannot say no to a woman stems from the age of three while living with his grandmother. She had told him to do what she said or she would send him home to his parents.

On February 7, 1991 Michael reported that he has accomplished very much toward changing his habits about not wanting to succeed. He is pleased about understanding the connections of the past and how they have changed the expressions in his present life.

From 1978 through 1980, with a five-year follow-up to those years, I was a researcher with the Parks Research and Education Project in Riverside California. In those first three years we saw over one thousand volunteers who came to evaluate why their medical problems were not responding to orthodox medical procedures.

The PREP research staff, in the beginning, consisted of twelve people. Five were in the final stages of their degree work at a local College. Another was a licensed Rolpher, one a school Guidance Administrator, two Social Workers, one a Master Hypnotist, and two Psychic Counselors. Early in the project both of the psychics, the rolpher, and one of the social workers left the program for various reasons. The others remained throughout the three years of active research. It was found the psychology majors, by using traditional methods of their professions, to an average of twenty-six one hour sessions to resolve or improve their client's problem. Using a method of hypnotic regression the others accomplished the same success in an average four one hour sessions.

The purpose of the project was to test the hypothesis that the mind is capable of healing the body of any physical or emotional illness by using hypnotic techniques. What the mind creates can be reversed by the same creative energy. However, individuals can't usually accomplish this balance without assistance.

I believe the subconscious mind has total knowledge of the individual's needs, drive, and motivations. It therefore follows that when communication has been established between the conscious and subconscious mind, there should be nothing about one's self that cannot be brought to the conscious level.

The Parks Research and Education Project provided evidence that man's mind does have the ability to heal the body when the cause of the problem is brought to the conscious awareness. And, with the use of hypnosis this awareness can be achieved in a very short time.

I don't recall why Jim came into the project but I do remember his hypnotic experience. During the session a fire engine went by the office with its sirens & horn blasting, causing my subject to come out of hypnosis. I enquired of him why this had startled him. He said that his parents had lived in Cuba. When his mother became pregnant with him she wanted him to be born in the United States. She was a full ten months into her pregnancy before she was able to come to the States. On her arrival here she was crossing a street and was struck by a fire engine and knocked to the ground. She was taken to a hospital where she gave birth to this son.

During the session he recalled a past life experience. At that moment he was an American pilot flying for the French in World War He was flying patrol over the front lines of the war. He said to me, "I'm trying to observe the enemy movements and keep this dam thing flying and you're talking to me". I stopped the session and awakened him from the trance. He said that while he was in that experience he had a very strong smell of Castor Oil. It was learned that Castor Oil was used to lubricate the engines of the airplanes of that time.

A friend I worked with for more than twenty years chose to retire from his job after being denied an expected promotion. One year after his retirement he went blind in his right eye. Exactly one year later his left eye failed. Doctors had told him they didn't know the cause of his blindness and couldn't help him. They suggested the arteries had become swollen and restricted the blood and oxygen to the vision systems. He tried acupuncture and other methods without success. In December of 1988 he asked me if hypnosis could determined the cause of his blindness.

At our first session we determined that emotion was behind the cause. Between December 1988 and April 1989 we had seventeen sessions without recording the results. These sessions seemed to connect with deaths occurring within his family and the endings of something in his life like his retirement. During these sessions physical and emotional changes occurred showing some progress in recovering his sight. He had incidents where he caught sight of certain objects and images but there was no constant vision. His expectation of recovering his sight brought about a better emotional attitude.

On April 13th, 1989 he reported that for the past five days "darkness" seemed to have set in and he was not even able to see shadows. A 15-minute session determined that the emotions of depression and impatience were responsible for this condition.

During these past sessions we evaluated the physical, emotional, and spiritual connections to his blindness. At this session a spirit entity told him to put his trust in Jesus, that he had something to learn that had to do with the future, and when the time was right he would be enlightened. At all of these sessions he felt close to recovering his sight. When his sight was not restored by a previous set deadline he did not experience remorse or doubt that what had taken place was a fantasy. He felt that things are happening and in time he would see again. These sessions still associated with past experiences of death in his family and other endings, like his retirement, not knowing what he was to do with the rest of his life.

On July 1, 1989 he was directed to mentally scan the vision systems to determine why his sight had not improved. He said it appeared to be in the frontal brain area where the nerves from the visual systems connected to the brain were not activated. This area was just behind the bridge of the nose and the center of the eyes. The nerves come from the eyes to an area about the size of a dime and then spread out into the brain. This area appeared to be gray in color and all around this area it appeared blood red. He said he had observed this area in a previous session and it had appeared to be black. When asked why the visual systems were not working he observed a hand and arm dressed in a robe come to him and say, "It's not time yet".

On September 14th, 1989 I had a friend, who reads palms, do an evaluation. He suggested that experiences at the ages of nine, eleven, and fifteen, had something to do with the eye problem. He also said the blindness appeared to be a part of destiny, but recovery was still possible.

In December we found a past life connection to his condition. He gave the year as 893 in the North of France. I was a healer and he was the victim of losing his sight. He had been struck in the face with a burning piece of wood. I had made a salve from herbs and roots, and after three or four months of treating his eyes he had recovered part of his sight. When asked why he was reliving the experience of blindness he said it was to teach him patience, trust, and faith. He said when he was at the age of forty he decided to have this experience and that he would recover from this blindness when he was near the age of sixty. He said that all of the vision and brain systems were in good health and that nothing needs to be done except activate the connection between the eye nerves and the brain in the system described.

At a session on April 28th, 1990 the problem spot appeared to have become compatible to the rest of the brain and looking good. He said he had already experienced instants of sight. He said that in the beginning process he had prayed to a Saint and then to the Mother Mary who moved him on to Christ. At one of the sessions he observed the hands of God holding two eyes and he now feels that the recovery of his sight is in the hands of God. Following the session he said that I was doing the right things to bring about the recovery of his sight, that I was his teacher bring him to a new spiritual awareness.

On August 27th, 1990 He visited a brother in Texas. While there he talked with a male psychic who told him the doctors would never recover his sight. But if he continued to meditate and pray he would recover his sight in 1991. The Psychic also confirmed the dates that emotional experiences had offended his sight, and these dates were the same as found in hypnotic regression, and from the reading of his palm by Abdullah.

On September 24th, 1991 the session brought the awareness of a spirit entity named John who was wearing a blue robe with a body length brown scarf around his neck and a white emblem on the left chest, with a cross and reversed "P" as a symbol of "The Keeper of the Keys of Knowledge". John told him the time was near for his sight to be restored, and in that instant he would understand the reason for the experience, that the sight would be restored as a spiritual expression and not physical.

On November 5th, 1991 a spirit entity dressed in a lavender robe, holding a book with loose leaf pages, with only three pages left to read, who told him the time is near to recover his sight, to have patience.

On February 8th, 1992 a spirit entity by the name of Joseph came to him with the pages. He was able to see there was only one paragraph left on a half page. The writing was in Arabic but he understood the meaning. A session on May 16th, 1992 displayed the pages of the book had all been turned and there was nothing more to be offered except time. A spirit entity named George appeared in a bright yellow light. George advised that my subject would become an inspiration to others but he still had a lot to learn.

My last session with this subject was on June 24, 1992. The spirit entity named John advised that the lessons had been learned and are now being tested. No time period was given concerning the recovery of his sight. Up to this time we had a total of 45 sessions, none lasting more than fifteen minutes.

After my friend became totally blind he had joined a class to learn the Braille system. In a very short time became a teacher of that subject. He was also selected to teach and lecture to other organizations for the blind. He became an inspiration to those who were also visually impaired. This duty lasted until his death on February 9, 1997 one month before reaching the age of 63. Remember he said he would recover his sight when he was near the age of sixty. Was this what was meant when he was told the recovery of his sight would be a spiritual experience and not physical?

My friend's wife was always present during these sessions. In the beginning she was concerned that this process was against her religious beliefs. It was only because of her husband's desire to try hypnotism that she went along with the idea. After a while she became more relaxed and interested in the sessions. A Priest friend, who was agreeable to the process, had come and put Holy Water on her husband's eyes. This also helped to ease her tension concerning her religious beliefs.

Since his death his wife has visited his crypt daily. She talks with him and he guides her in making her choices and decisions. He gives her names of items she needs, names she has never heard of before. He wanted to buy her a new car before he died. When her car became too expensive to repair she drove to a new car dealership but couldn't make a decision about buying. She asked for a sign to help her decide. When she went to leave the dealers lot she, and others, couldn't get her car started. She took this as a sign from her husband and bought a new 2001 Saturn.

The CBS television program, 60-minutes, of December 1, 2000 had a segment by a Doctor Farwell of which he calls "Brain Fingerprinting" suggesting that the brain cannot recall anything it hasn't experienced. For over forty years I have been suggesting that the brain has recorded everything it has experienced and can recall this information through the process of hypnotic regression. There is an expression called False Memory Syndrome. This refers to the fact that a person can lie while in the state of hypnosis, and the mind can be contaminated by suggestions that are not true. However, the truth of an experience is still there as it was originally recorded, and this truth can be recovered by my method of hypnotherapy. I predict that the material in this book will be questioned and/or rejected because of the impact to the medical & psychology professions who reject hypnotism as a means of correcting physical, emotional, and spiritual problems. The problem is that results or success by the use of hypnosis cannot be predicted because of the difference in the beliefs and of the personalities involved.

Chapter Sixteen
THEORIES AND CONCLUSIONS

In contemplating the format of this final chapter it is my desire that the material in this book will add to the proof that a link, or association, does exist between the physical life of man and the spiritual realm from which we came. Hypnotism is a means of making us aware of this connection and of bringing out the powers which heal our physical, emotional and spiritual ills. Recognizing this source of power within us is a means of fulfilling the will of God. A close review of the information given by those in the attitude of hypnotic regression proves there is an inner knowledge which transcends the comprehension of the individual's conscious awareness.

Consider hypnotic regression and its reference to reincarnation and the communication between the spiritual and physical worlds. Where else can we look for other proofs of these conditions? The Bible is one source. In this book there are many different references to spirit communication and the philosophy of reincarnation. My favorite passage concerning the re-cycle of life is in John 3:4 where Jesus debated with Nicodemus about the question, "How can a man be born when he is old? Can he enter the second time into his mother's womb and be born?" I can only suggest that if you are in doubt about the great question of life and death, study the Bible. Take a good look at the life around you, learn, and most of all, prove the spiritual laws as laid out in the Bible by living them.

This re-cycle of the soul, from the spiritual world to the physical, again and again, within the allotted time of this era, is God's way of allowing man to prove to himself the divine laws of the universe. By belief and action the soul retains it's immortality and eternal life

Reincarnation is not just a theory. It is a definite set of laws which directly affect the mortality of all human beings and their soul. By developing his mental attributes toward sociological improvement, as well as biological, man will understand the concepts of reincarnation and, in the future, will accept it as fact. What better means do we have of learning this knowledge than by the process of prayer, meditation, or hypnotic regression? By desire and these methods contact is made with the soul and spirit and its responses to the purpose of living in the physical.

The understanding I gained from these hypnotic expressions I have observed, is that we were created, in spirit, in the likeness of God, then given a set of rules, or laws, compatible to the nature of our respective creation. We were given free agency (freedom of choice) to deny, challenge, test, or conform to these laws. As the result of our (mankind) choice to be not obedient to these laws, we fell from the Grace of God to the level of our knowledge and expression of them and have since been in the process of returning to our source.

God gave to man the power of reason for the purpose of enabling him to successfully struggle with his physical environment. He gave him the power to know right from wrong, and He gave him supreme control of the initial process of reasoning, thus making him responsible for the moral status of his soul. God made man a free moral agent and man can express this "Free Agency" for as long as he wishes but, until he conforms to the laws of his Creator, he must experience and re-experience those conditions where he is in violation of these laws.

All life, whatever it is, and wherever it is, has a physical beginning and ending. With each life journey it tries to evolve to a better expression than that of its prior incarnations. Every life form, being in the same process, needs the help of its environment to grow and become a stronger, wiser, and better species. We must learn that it is better to help one another toward these goals than create competition to destroy, or take advantage of, the weak.

We will all get together sometime. Each experience is to teach us to live together in harmony. We are all one. All races are the same. Over time they have adjusted to their environment. Adam and Eve represent man and woman. We are all brothers and sisters.

Dying is like being born and being born is like dying. What we call death is only a transition into another dimension of awareness. People think they go someplace else when they die but, in reality, they just change their level of existence. They don't go anywhere. When we die we absorb all that we have experienced then slowly, after a period of time we desire again to repeat a life experience on earth. We can feel this. It's rather like wanting something but not knowing what it is. We are able to discuss this wanting with God and then make arrangements to try to fit ourselves into a pattern which will satisfy this yearning, this need we have.

With man's "Free Agency" an individual may choose to be born to experience confinement. This can be experienced by a life in the military, jail or a hospital. We can experience this confinement as the patient/nurse or jailer/inmate, etc.

My subject, Rebecca, was asked how she felt about predestination. She replied, "Yes, things just don't happen, things are planned. Every life that is taken is planned. No matter how it happens, everything is planned. Most things are planned so you can learn. If you leave a place and go to another, it is so you can learn. You have your free agency and ability to reason. You don't have to take that trip. I'm not saying they are planned, say a hundred years before they happen, but they are planned as you go along. Everything you do, even if you just scratch your head, it's all recorded, every bit, even when you are asleep".

A male adult, in regression, responded to a question about predestination in this way. "At every given moment infinite possibilities are possible and yet, only one becomes actual and, at that stage of becoming actual, one could say that it's predestined. Before that, nothing is predestined".

The Bible tells us, "Whom He did predestine, them He also called; and whom He called, them He also glorified" (Romans 8:30).

"Having predestined us, being predestined according to the purpose of Him who worketh all things after the counsel of His will" (Ephesians 1:5).

Reference is made in the documented records of Edgar Cayce to the word and laws of "Karma". Karma, in Webster's Dictionary, is defined as, "Totality of a person's actions in one of the successive states of his existence, thought of as determining his fate in the next".

When one consults the Bible, as in Matthew 7:12, one reads: "Judge not that ye be not judged; for with what judgment ye judge, ye shall be judged; and with what measure ye mete, it shall be measured to you again." We can also relate this passage with a penalty, or a gift, depending on the expression of the individual. In hypnotic regression the entity does not look at these conditions as a penalty. It is a free choice of the individual to place himself in an experience that will give him a better understanding of a past action. As an example; A common practice in the past was the use of a hot poker to burn out the eyes of an enemy. One who has done this would resolve his

Karma by being born blind, or by being in the service of a blind person, so he can better understand his past action.

Doctor Franz Hartman in his, <u>Life of Paracelsus</u>, says: "Men do not think what they choose, but that which comes into their minds. If they could control the action of their minds, they would be able to control their own nature, and nature by which their forms are surrounded". This can and is being done, but only by God and the belief thereof.

Doctor C. Thompson in his, <u>Systems of Psychology</u>, says, "I have had a feeling of the uselessness of all voluntary effort, and also that the matter was working itself clear in my mind. It has many times seemed to me that I was really a passive instrument in the hands of a person not myself".

"When I watch the flowing river which, out of regions I see not, pours for a season its stream into me, I see that I am not a cause, but a surprised spectator of this ethereal water" (Emerson).

There is nothing we do not know about ourselves on the subconscious level. Within each of us is the awareness of our own spiritual growth, a level of spiritual knowledge, the number of past lives it has taken us to get to our respective levels, and the purpose for which we came into our physical experience. With the process of hypnosis these levels can be experienced.

The concept of reincarnation is always present regardless of our conscious beliefs. I have found that those who choose to be agnostics or atheists have the same spiritual awareness in the subconscious as those who practice a religion and belief in God. This, of course, is compatible to their own spiritual level. I find those at levels below three do not believe in reincarnation. The mind is saying that reincarnation does not exist until one believes it. This, again, is our freedom of choice. When individuals experiences their level, they become aware of their choice to stay where they are or raise themselves to higher levels.

One man told me that he was at spiritual level four and had lived thirty-seven past lives. Another man told me he was at spiritual level twenty-six and had lived only four past lives. This is a rare occurrence so I asked how he was able to reach such a high level in only four past lives. His response was, "By listening to my father". Meaning listening to God.

If reincarnation is real, and it is, it means every human being in this physical expression for a pre-determined purpose. That purpose is to learn who we are, where we came from, where we are going, and what is the best way to get there. If everyone could recognize this truth what a wonderful experience we would be having in helping each other to accomplish this goal.

Negative emotions such as resentment, anger, hate, etc, not only restrict us from raising ourselves to higher spiritual levels they are also harmful to our own physical and emotional systems.

Years of contact with the spiritual realm have produced several comments of which many have stayed with me. Some of these follow;

"Now I am beyond. Beyond your world. Beyond your comprehension."

"We come from spirit and we return to spirit. Earth is a proving ground to establish choices relating to the laws of our creation.

We need to come down in order to go up. This means that in helping, or working, or doing things for other people below us, we can go higher. We can solve problems. We have to come down in order to go up."

"Do you know what is meant by the higher and lower self? I am what I am, but I have a reflection of what I am. In time, we become the same."

"I enjoy talking to you because you force me to reach further up to get the answers which I probably would not do otherwise. It's hard for us to grow by ourselves. We need the energy that you bring us. I get a real good feeling talking to you."

'We do not have the emotions you have. We have to study this. We have reached a point where we have sadness for others. We are happy for ourselves."

"We had a war here, but not a war of weapons. This was a verbal war between Christ and Satan to determine who would come to your world to get the people to follow their doctrine. God arbitrated this war and decided Christ would be the one to come to your world. If more people could experience the contact with their Souls it would change the whole world."

Think about what would happen if everyone followed the Bible instruction of Matthew 7:12. "And as ye would that man should do to you, do ye also to them likewise."

In an early regression I was told "We operate around a pole, a positive and negative pole within ourselves. We have energy that is seen as light. The mind, body and spirit are different levels of vibration, like a circle within a circle, broader, wider, or bigger. The aura is the outer vibrations of the body, beyond perhaps, what you would consider the outer limit of the body. We just have a circle of light with a center. It's the same in essence except the body is a lower vibration. Life on other planets is basically the same. It is a polarity with a center and a sphere, and that's what we are, a center and a sphere with a source of energy".

Some people have a natural ability to see the aura's of the body. One day while I was working with a lady, using hypnosis, her friend observed and became frightened because she saw a field of purple light emanating from my hands as I moved them about the lady's head. This was an ability the lady didn't know she had.

One of the greatest prophets of modern time was Edgar Cayce (1877-1945). This man, through applied and self-hypnosis, could display powers of telepathy and clairvoyance far beyond many others in modern times. He became known as, "The Sleeping Prophet", a medical diagnostician and religious seer in addition to being a professional photographer. In 1932, a foundation known as the "Association For Research and Enlightenment" (A.R.E.), was founded to preserve the records and documents of the history of Mr. Cayce's psychic perceptions. From these records many books have been written about his psychic interpretations of reincarnation, prophecy, dreams, and advanced medical knowledge. Review of the Cayce material will give the reader a better understanding and evaluation of my material.

Christ declared that the most essential condition for healing the sick is faith, not only in the patient, but also in the healer. Another condition, which was a part of His healing process was to establish a favorable mental environment. Having a positive mental force surrounding the patient, or subject, is as important in hypnotism as in other methods of healing. An atmosphere of interest and belief brings very positive reactions while the adverse influence caused by doubt and skepticism of those present restricts the performance of the subject and the operator alike.

Attempting to teach that Christ worked within natural law to heal the sick is as futile today as it was in His time. I have tried to show that by following this law of belief we are all capable of healing the sick and bringing about miracles just as did Jesus. For example, when given the truth about the simplicity of hypnotism people seem to lose respect for its power the same as they lost their faith in the power of God when they thought Christ worked within these natural laws. The laws of hypnotism are just as much a part of our nature as Christ's laws were of His. There can be no doubt about our power to heal.

The injunction that Christ gave to those He healed, "See thou tell no man", is another important condition involving the use of hypnotism today. When a person is suddenly healed, or helped, by a mental process it becomes very important that he not talk about the healing to persons who are skeptical. The reason is that the skeptic, in his endeavor to dispute the facts or ridicule the idea that such a process is effective, causes the subject to question his own faith. If this negative attitude is maintained it will eventually cause their doubts and fears to be realized. The laws of faith, when applied to the power to heal the sick, are the same laws that govern the soul in its relation to eternal life.

Christ proclaimed that belief is a condition precedent to immortal life. Therefore, in the absence of this belief the soul cannot relate to its conscious existence. A soul thus being saved by belief in immortality then answers in the body by rewards and/or punishment. The laws of cause and effect are very real. "God will render to every man according to his deeds; to them who by patient continuance in well doing seek for glory and honor and immortality, eternal life" (Romans 2:6-7).

In Chapter One, were listed three levels of consciousness which make up the different mind systems. I suggested that our best attitude or expression is when we get these three mind systems to think and act alike, recognizing the super-conscious as the strongest and more real. In other words, we need to be our own independent selves and function at our own level of spiritual growth. All physical, emotional, and spiritual stress seems to come from the difference between what we do (conscious level) and what we are (subconscious level). It has been said that if everyone obeyed just one of the Ten Commandments it would change our entire world for the better.

I suppose the big question about this book will be; "Do you really believe that you talked to God and Christ in the regressions with the Leader and Teacher"? The answer is YES! Who can truly judge such an experience except those directly involved or those who have had such an experience themselves? By my works, thoughts, and actions, I hope to prove the truth of my experience.

"Your only assurance of a personal God consists in your own insight as to your belief in, and experience with, things spiritual. To all your fellows who have had a similar experience, no argument about the personality, or reality, of God is necessary, while to all other men, who are not thus sure of God, no possible argument could ever be truly convincing". The Urantia Book, page 1107

If I believe all of this, and I conduct myself in the suggested attitudes and purpose, it can't hurt me if it is not true. But if I do not believe it and reject this knowledge it can do a great deal of harm if it is true. Some people want to learn and others want proof. It is knowledge not proof that is important.

As I think of ways to compare my work with others, in order that the reader can better evaluate this material, I think of my own attitude when confronted with my visits with the Leader and Teacher. I wanted great signs and more substantial proof that the experiences were real. I now realize that I was of the same mind as the people of Christ's time who continued to demand more proof of His powers. "Except ye see signs and wonders, ye will not believe." (St. John 4:48)

In summarizing these concepts of hypnotic regression, as I have come to understand them, the following pattern is established:

The argument that man evolved from a single organism of plant or animal is only speculation and theory. That man was a special creation of a supreme power (God) there is no doubt. Archaeological finds of ancient sacred records throughout the world all refer to the origin of man as a special creation, endowed with an imperishable spirit and a supreme mentality, with mystic powers to rule the earth in the manner of his creation. Man, upon his creation, was given the spirit of God and a free moral agency. He was instructed in the right and lawful things of life and, when man learns to obey these instructions and how to make use of his soul force, he will overcome the evils and influences of the material and ascend to his pre-ordained goal, the control of the forces and elements of the Earth. Man's soul is immortal in its existence in the physical body but, because of the disobedience of God's laws, he must experience suffering and death until, by his own efforts, he can bring himself to accept and conform to the divine laws of God.

. There is an underlying truth which remains constant. This is that the source of all power is mind. The processes of hypnotism, prayer, and meditation are means of exercising the power of the mind toward a predetermined goal. Within this spiritual creation, called man, is the knowledge of that spiritual creation and its purpose.

Throughout my experiences in hypnotic regression when in contact with spiritual entities, I continually ask, "Why is this happening to me"? The response is usually, "You must be privileged". I reflect back to my youth and recall conditions of illness and other experiences, which would usually result in death. I also recall my attitudes when offered opportunities to get involved in activities that were considered sinful or unlawful. I refused these activities with the thought that God was saving me for something better. It was not until my involvement with hypnotism, and my experiences therein, that I felt that this must be what I had been preparing for. It is my interest and desire to continue teaching that which I have learned and to someday become a spiritual healer. I have been given instructions toward this goal by the regression process. Astrology, palmistry, psychic awareness, and hypnotic regression have confirmed this purpose and I have had some very satisfying experiences in these expressions of mind. With patience and desire, and most of all by living the ways of nature's laws, I expect to reach my goal.

The following is a list of principles by which are always present and consistent in the spiritual realm of the mind.

1. The law of cause and effect is universal. Every act creates a consequence and we reap that which we sow.

2. In the final analysis, we are responsible only for ourselves. We are created as unique and independent entities with the freedom of choice. Therefore, we are responsible for our own choices and actions. We create our own realities.

3. We have no right to control or coerce another person. We have our free will and the mechanism of choice as does everyone. We must allow others their learning choices.

4. There is no right or wrong. Everything is relevant and purposeful. Experience tends to be absolute and not relative. Circumstances, and their effects on the individual, are self-contained within the individual. That which is meaningful in experience for a particular individual is retained and determines what he is and becomes.

5. All physical and emotional pain signals a problem which needs attention. All physical and emotional problems are the result of negative emotions if these emotions have not been resolved within a reasonable time.

6. Man's highest achievement is unconditional love and service. We are all in the same boat. A goal exists toward which we are evolving, and a value standard is perceived with the goal being the highest value against which all other values are measured.

That goal is to return to our source (God) and become that which we have always been. Regardless of our sex, nationality, or religion, there is no difference in this process. These are expressions we choose to experience for the recovery of the knowledge given to us at our creation.

What happens when we get there?

You cease to be,
And yet you are,
As you become,
That, which you have always been.

Freedom of choice, we reap what we sow; cause & effect, the Golden Rule, and the Ten Commandments are laws of our creation that cannot and will not be denied.

ABOUT THE AUTHOR

A.L.Ward was born in Tarkio Missouri, educated in schools in California, served with the Navy on aircraft duty, 1943-1945, and on returning obtained a commercial pilot's license with flight instructors rating. He joined the San Bernardino Police Department in 1955, a duty he shared with three brothers and a sister in the same department. He is a member of the Masonic orders, Scottish Rite and Shrine.

Mr. Ward lists golf and bowling among his hobbies and had maintained a master rating on the police pistol team. A long time interest in hypnotism led him to several years of study with a master hypnotist, and he was one of the first to use this science in police service. He has lectured on hypnosis, regression therapy and other mind dynamics at schools, colleges, private organizations and service clubs, and has appeared several time on television. In 1996 the National Guild of Hypnotists gave him the Ormond McGill award for presenter of the year.

He was selected to assist in the Parks Research and Education Project from 1977 through 1980. This research explored the use of hypnosis in documented medical problems that were not responding to orthodox medical procedures. From this research he developed a method of exploring the origin, cause, and solution of any physical, emotional or spiritual problem in a one-hour hypnotic session.

Printed in the United States
47118LVS00005B/220-270

9 781403 387615